KU-316-200

The
Person-centred
approach to therapeutic change

Michael McMillan

HALESOWEN COLLEGE
LIBRARY

Los Angeles | London | New Delhi
Singapore | Washington DC

© Michael McMillan 2004

First published 2004
Reprinted 2009, 2010

Apart from any fair dealing for the purposes of research or
private study, or criticism or review, as permitted under the
Copyright, Designs and Patents Act, 1988, this publication
may be reproduced, stored or transmitted in any form, or by
any means, only with the prior permission in writing of the
publishers, or in the case of reprographic reproduction, in
accordance with the terms of licences issued by the
Copyright Licensing Agency. Enquiries concerning
reproduction outside those terms should be sent to
the publishers.

SAGE Publications Ltd
Oliver's Yard
55 City Road
London EC1Y 1SP

SAGE Publications Inc.
2455 Teller Road
Thousand Oaks, California 91320

SAGE Publications India Pvt Ltd
B 1/I 1 Mohan Cooperative Industrial Area
Mathura Road
New Delhi 110 044

SAGE Publications Asia-Pacific Pte Ltd
33 Pekin Street #02-01
Far East Square
Singapore 048763

British Library Cataloguing in Publication data

A catalogue record for this book is available from the British
Library

ISBN 978 0 7619 4868 1
ISBN 978 0 7619 4869 8 (pbk)

Library of Congress Control Number: 2003115332

FSC
Mixed Sources
Product group from well-managed
forests and other controlled sources
Cert no. SGS-COC-2953
www.fsc.org
© 1996 Forest Stewardship Council

Typeset by C&M Digitals (P) Ltd, Chennai, India
Printed in Great Britain by CPI Antony Rowe, Chippenham, Wiltshire

Coun

The

Person-centred

approach to therapeutic change

059341

Sage Therapeutic Change Series

Books in the *Sage Therapeutic Change Series* examine 'change' as the goal of counselling and psychotherapy. Each book takes a different therapeutic approach and looks at how change is conceptualised and worked with by practitioners from that approach. Giving examples which demonstrate how theory and principles are put into practice, the books are suitable for both trainee and experienced counsellors and psychotherapists.

Series Editor: Windy Dryden

Books in the series:

The Rational Emotive Behavioural Approach to Therapeutic Change
Windy Dryden & Michael Neenan

The Psychodynamic Approach to Therapeutic Change
Rob Leiper & Michael Maltby

The Person-Centred Approach to Therapeutic Change
Michael McMillan

Contents

OJ9341
361. 323 MAN
CounJEWING
CUC

Foreword by Dave Mearns

It is an honour to be asked to write a foreword for this new book by Michael McMillan. I have been excited about this book ever since I read early drafts of its first two chapters some time ago at the birth of the project. At different times thereafter I have read other parts and my consistent impression has been that this is an author who has both a sophisticated academic understanding of the material and a great skill in communicating that widely. Those two qualities do not often go together!

The book is about *change*. After a first chapter in which the author introduces us to the person-centred concept of the person, Chapter 2 is devoted to the change process within the client, including a very accessible description of Rogers' *process model*. Chapter 3 goes on to explore why and how change occurs in the human being, while Chapter 4 introduces the most up-to-date person-centred theory in relation to the nature of the self-concept and its changing process. Chapters 5 and 6 explore why change occurs in therapy and the conditions that facilitate that change, while Chapter 7 looks beyond the core conditions to focus on the particular quality of *presence*, begging the question as to whether this is a transpersonal/transcendental quality or an intense experiencing of the core conditions themselves.

This is an intensely *modern* book, particularly in its postmodern emphasis. Rogers is sometimes characterised as coming from modernist times but he can also be seen as one of the early postmodernists in his emphasis on process more than outcome and relationship more than personal striving. The modern nature of the book is also emphasised by a superb analysis of the relationship between focusing and person-centred therapy in Chapter 5, linking also with Polanyi's notion of *indwelling* in this and other chapters. In suggesting that in both focusing and person-centred therapy the therapist is inviting the client to 'indwell' him or herself, the author provides a framework for considering many modern perceptions of the approach including notions such as 'presence' and 'relational depth'. Also, the link with focusing is modern in the sense that the present World Association for the approach covers a fairly broad family including traditional person-centred therapists, experiential therapists, focusing-oriented therapists and process-guiding therapists. Important in this development is the kind of dialogue encouraged by the present book.

Within the World Association, one of the most notable features is the strength of the modern British School. More than any other text, this book introduces us to a range of the newer British academics working on the theory and practice of person-centred therapy, people such as Cooper, Haugh, Moore, Tudor, Wilkins, Worrall and Wyatt (all referenced in the text). It is refreshing to read these writers reviewed in the present text as well as those from an earlier generation. It will be fascinating to see what they, including Michael McMillan, will create for the future of person-centred therapy.

Dave Mearns
September 2003

Several years ago there was a series of jokes doing the rounds with the question 'How many "x" does it take to change a light bulb?' The one I remember finding most appealing was, 'How many psychotherapists does it take to change a light bulb?' Answer: 'Only one, but it has to really want to change.' As with many classic jokes, it works so well because it satirises what many people consider to be true. But what the joke implies, perhaps unintentionally, is that the notion of change is central to the activity of psychotherapy.

Now, years have gone by and there has been much debate about the interchangeability of the terms 'psychotherapy' and 'counselling'. (Indeed, I will use the terms interchangeably throughout this book, a convention that previously was not so acceptable.) But the principle remains unaltered for this therapeutic activity, whatever the term used to describe it: change happens! At least, that is the intention of most of the work undertaken in the name of therapy, even if it is not successful. Most schools of thought within the counselling field have evolved out of the desire to facilitate change, an outcome that is generally hoped to be in some way or other positive, whatever the description of 'positive' might be. Even those therapists who do not explicitly claim 'change' as their goal would not deny, I suspect, that some change occurs during or as a result of the therapeutic relationship.

Given the centrality, then, of the notion of change to the activity of counselling, what this book offers is a description and exploration of the theory and practice of person-centred counselling, with particular reference to the notion of change and how and why it occurs during the process of counselling. Perhaps more than any other theoretical orientation, the person-centred approach places the notion of change at the very centre of its conception of the psychologically healthy person. While other therapies may attempt to facilitate a person's cognitive reordering from 'wrong' thought to 'right' thought, or perhaps a more holistic transformation from being person A to person B, person-centred theory hypothesises something fundamentally more radical: that to exist in a constant state of change is in fact the goal. Indeed, this is perhaps too radical, even for some who would probably align themselves with the person-centred approach.

Although in theory the notion of a person being in a constant state of change may seem a little nonsensical, the reality is not so bizarre. For what this notion of constant change underpins is a concept that is not so unusual – a concept of an unconditional acceptance of oneself. The person who can achieve an unconditional self-acceptance or *unconditional positive self-regard*, as Rogers described it, will be fluid and ever-changing because their development will never be curtailed by external value-judgements as to what is right or wrong. External value-judgements or *conditions of worth*, which can lead to a highly complex as well as a rigid self-concept (as described in Chapters 3 and 4), are what prevent the client from being open to experience and therefore change. (These and other terms will be clarified throughout the book.) Thus a person who is free of their conditions of worth will continually change in whatever way they feel best fulfils their needs in light of their experience. This is not to suggest that the person will become oblivious to the needs of others, a criticism that has been levelled at the person-centred approach (see Chapter 2). It is simply proposing that the most constructive development will occur where the person does not need to defend themselves against their experience and so is free to adapt and change uninhibitedly.

A liberation from the fear and anxiety that experiencing can provoke is what the person-centred approach is suggesting is possible. Fundamental to that liberation, and therefore to the practice of person-centred counselling, is a trust in the nature of human beings. This means that, given the right therapeutic conditions, clients will be able to make decisions about how best to maintain and enhance themselves as they develop an increased sense of self-acceptance. This book outlines the theoretical framework on which such a trust is based and describes how the framework informs person-centred practice. The emphasis within practice is not so much on doing something *to* the client as being *with* the client in a facilitative manner, hence the notion of *indwelling* the client and offering 'the core conditions' (see Chapters 5 and 6). Thus the ethos of the counselling relationship is one of facilitating client self-acceptance: it is only through this that the client can move toward the enhancing existence of ever-changingness.

This is such a simple notion and yet, half a century on from when Rogers first developed his theory, it still has profound consequences for the person and their ability to maintain and enhance themselves. An openness to experience because of a self-acceptant attitude means the person can adapt and change to whatever experience is encountered. The profound sense of freedom arising out of this shift away from defensiveness towards openness in relation to *all* experience is certainly an enticing prospect and one that would seem to offer a genuinely new way of being. Even in today's society, when perhaps more than ever before we are confronted by conditions of worth through the media and the complexities of modern-day living (see Chapter 8), Rogers' notion of a continual changingness seems entirely valid and appropriate. Indeed, this simple notion perhaps offers a pathway into the future as our society becomes increasingly complex and psychologically demanding.

Hopefully this book will aid anyone seeking to clarify how and why change occurs from a person-centred perspective. Rogers did not intend his hypotheses to be taken as fact and applied rigidly within the counselling relationship, forcing client experience to fit theoretical construct. Similarly, this book is intended to provide a deeper understanding of the process of change that can be used to inform counselling practice, not define and curtail it. Offering a counselling relationship within the person-centred approach can be an extremely demanding undertaking, as discussed in Chapter 6. Approaching such a relationship with a clear working map of the process can be a useful preparation for the endeavour ahead, as long as it remains just that – a working map that is a rough guide to be continually updated. Hopefully that is what this book can provide – a working map of the process of change which can be continually updated.

The person-centred approach is often criticised for being somewhat lacking in theoretical complexity. Carl Rogers, the founder of person-centred (originally 'client-centred') therapy, is dismissed by many as being too simplistic or just plain naive in his attempts to describe and explain the psychological development of the person (for example, Masson, 1989). Indeed, the person-centred approach has sometimes been caricatured as being at the 'tea and sympathy' end of the psychotherapy spectrum. Such caricature is somewhat surprising given that Rogers, particularly in his earlier work, writes in an exact and scientific language. People are 'organisms'; terminology is painstakingly categorised and described; complex diagrams meticulously delineate psychological relationships. Rogers' use of language did change as he grew older, with a decrease in the use of terms common to scientific psychology, perhaps reflecting the fading of the influences he experienced early on in his life and career (Thorne, 1992). But despite this change he remained consistent with his original statements of theory regarding the person and their development, seemingly not feeling the need for any major revisions.

His exposition of relatively simple ideas is not necessarily one that is insubstantial and he would no doubt agree with the statement that 'simplicity is not a goal, but one arrives at simplicity in spite of oneself, as one approaches the real meaning of things' (Lewis, 1974: 20). Any suggestion that his theory is lightweight, however, would seem misplaced; his theory of psychological maladjustment has at its centre a simple hypothesis but this does not mean it is lacking in substance and rigorous analysis. Indeed, Rogers describes his ideas in quite some detail and many other writers have commented on and revised his work as well (see the Further Reading sections at the end of each chapter). A lengthy investigation of his theoretical framework, therefore, is not required here, although a summary of the fundamental principles of his theory is essential to the consideration of how change occurs as a result of the counselling process.

The actualising tendency

At the centre of Rogers' theory is the notion of an *actualising tendency*. He postulates that 'there is a formative directional tendency in the universe, which can be traced and observed in stellar space, in crystals, in micro-organisms, in more complex organic life, and in human beings' (Rogers, 1980: 133). The actualising tendency, the term most often used when referring to this formative tendency in human beings, is 'the inherent tendency of the organism to develop all its capacities in ways which serve to maintain or enhance the organism' (Rogers, 1959: 198). It is absolutely fundamental to life, to the extent that Rogers remarks, 'only the presence or absence of this total directional process enables us to tell whether a given organism is alive or dead' (Rogers, 1980: 118). Crucially it is the only motive that Rogers presents in his understanding of human life; it incorporates all other motivational concepts such as tension or drive-reductions that are often differentiated in other theories. The actualising tendency is, however, concerned with increasing tension, as the organism is in a constant state of enhancement (Bozarth and Brodley, 1991); in any case, all directional motives are incorporated in this one tendency.

For Rogers, this inherent and unceasing tendency for all organisms to fulfil and enhance their potential is encapsulated in a memory he has about potatoes. Potatoes would not seem to be the most dynamic example to elucidate the central thesis of a theory on human development but these potatoes proved to Rogers that the actualising tendency would remain present even under the most adverse of circumstances. Interestingly, he observed, it would not be extinguished but it could be distorted:

> I remember that in my boyhood, the bin in which we stored our winter's supply of potatoes was in the basement, several feet below a small window. The conditions were unfavorable, but the potatoes would begin to sprout – pale white sprouts, so unlike the healthy green shoots they sent up when planted in the soil in the spring. But these sad, spindly sprouts would grow 2 or 3 feet in length as they reached toward the distant light of the window. The sprouts were, in their bizarre, futile growth, a sort of desperate expression of the directional tendency I have been describing. They would never become plants, never mature, never fulfill their real potential. But under the most adverse circumstances, they were striving to become. (Rogers, 1980: 118)

Thus this memory highlights two important factors: the tendency towards enhancement cannot be destroyed unless the organism itself is destroyed because it simply *exists* within it; but the organism's tendency towards enhancement can be distorted under adverse conditions. This first aspect is fundamental to the whole ethos of the person-centred approach and is integral to any consideration of how change occurs: the actualising tendency is innate and permeates the whole organism, not just one or other part of it. It is continually trying to maintain and enhance the organism as a whole and as it wants for nothing but the maintenance and enhancement of the organism, it is entirely trustworthy. It is not something that requires anything 'doing' to it in order for it to work – it just *is*. The second aspect is also important, as will become clear in this chapter, because it underlines the fact that the tendency is susceptible to adverse conditions and so growth and development can become distorted.

Trusting the organismic valuing process

Rogers thought of this tendency within living beings as a kind of *organismic valuing process* and found evidence of its existence in babies in the way they acted upon their instinctual needs (Rogers, 1973). He found that in experiments where babies were allowed to choose between a variety of foods on offer, the infants made choices based on what they needed to maintain and enhance their own well-being and growth. They would balance their intake of proteins, carbohydrates and vitamins to match their body's needs; if they ate too much of something they would soon stop and counteract the effect by eating a different food group. Rogers thought that the babies could not have learned this – it was evidence of their innate internal valuing process occurring uninhibitedly.

With reference to the therapeutic setting, Rogers believes that trusting in this innate valuing process is central to the activity of counselling. Thus it 'is not a matter of doing something to the individual, or of inducing him to do something about himself. It is instead a matter of freeing him for normal growth and development' (Rogers, 1942: 29). Rogers' memory of the potato sprouts is, for him, comparable to his work with clients whose lives have been 'warped' by adverse circumstances (1980: 118). Although some of these people's behaviours may seem 'abnormal, twisted, scarcely human', Rogers views these people as striving to enhance themselves in the best ways that are available to them (1980: 119). Even though this may produce somewhat distorted results, the actualising tendency is clearly still present within them and can continue to be trusted. This fundamental trust in the person is a startlingly different stance from that taken by many other therapies, where the emphasis is on in some way constraining rather than liberating the essence of human nature. In these therapies the essence is viewed as at least partly destructive as opposed to wholly constructive.

Rogers has come under criticism for what many believe to be his naive view of human nature (for example, Masson, 1989; Spinelli, 2000; and perhaps most famously, May, 1990). May (1990) described in some detail why he thought Rogers' view of an essentially 'good' human nature was misconceived, arguing in a similar way to Buber (Buber and Rogers, 1960) that there must be both good and evil present within all human beings. Rogers' response to May was emphatic: 'I feel that the tendency toward actualization is inherent. In this, man is like all other organisms. I can count on it being present ... I find in my experience no such tendency toward destructiveness, toward evil. I cannot count on the certainty that this individual is striving consciously or unconsciously to fulfill an evil nature' (Rogers, 1990b: 253). As Spinelli (2000) comments, Rogers may have subsequently wanted to add to the answer he gave to May at that time because it was in some ways inadequate, but Rogers' fundamental view of the actualising tendency being the enhancing source of human nature did not alter. Even as late as 1986 Rogers, when reflecting on the significant elements of a counselling session with a client, Jan, wrote of 'a trust in the "wisdom of the organism" to lead us to the core of her problems ... when trusted, her organism, her nonconscious mind – call it what you will – can follow the path that leads to the crucial issues' (Rogers, 1990a: 151). Implicit within this was his belief that once identified, Jan would also be able to address 'the crucial issues' in the best possible way for herself. Thus his trust in the person remained an integral element of the therapeutic relationship: change may occur, not because of what the counsellor does to the client but rather as a result of the counsellor liberating what already exists within the client.

This is exemplified by three filmed interviews conducted by Rogers and other leading therapists of the time (Fritz Perls and Albert Ellis) with a client called Gloria (Shostrom, 1964). Immediately after the sessions, Gloria comments that if she were beginning therapy she would choose to work with Rogers, but in her current state she thought the challenging style of Perls would be of most help. However, Rogers actually met Gloria a year or so after the filmed interviews had taken place, when she came to a conference he was running at which the participants watched the film of Gloria's sessions. Rogers reports that on seeing the session of herself with Perls she was clearly distressed, exclaiming 'Why did I do all those things that he asked me to do! Why did I let him do that to me!' (Rogers, 1984: 424). Rogers comments: 'She felt that she had somehow given over her power and this enraged her' (1984: 424). Rogers, of course, had not 'asked' Gloria to do anything in his session with her, he had simply trusted her to lead the way in their exploration of her situation, believing in the client's ability to find her own ways and means of overcoming her difficulties. It seems that ultimately his way of being with her was of greater value. Thus, the person-centred counsellor, with their trust firmly in the capabilities of the client and their capacity for change, can perhaps best be thought of as attempting to facilitate a reunion: the re-connection of the self with the client's inherent capabilities.

The self and unconditional positive regard

How, then, does this actualising tendency become distorted in people – how is the internal valuing process affected when subjected to adverse circumstances? This is another aspect that is central to Rogers' theory and involves two key concepts: *the self* and *unconditional positive regard*. Rogers (1951), in an attempt to clarify his thinking about personality and behaviour, presented his hypotheses at the time in the form of 19 propositions, and number nine offers a succinct description of his understanding of the 'self':

As a result of interaction with the environment, and particularly as a result of evaluational interaction with others, the structure of self is formed – an organized, fluid, but consistent conceptual pattern of perceptions of characteristics and relationships of the 'I' or the 'me,' together with values attached to these concepts. (Rogers, 1951: 498)

Here, Rogers hypothesises that due to a child's interaction with their environment, and particularly through their interaction with other people, they develop a sense of their own 'self'. Within the child there now exists the actualising tendency as before, which the child experiences (without consciously thinking about it) through their own organismic valuing process. But there is also an element of awareness that is conceptualised as 'self', which is, at its simplest, an awareness of being in existence. As this concept of self gradually develops, the child increasingly comes to be valued by (and in relation to) the other people around them and the child wants to actualise this *self-concept* as well as continuing to have their own organismic valuing process. This is a major shift in the child's development as now, in effect, there is a sub-system of the actualising tendency: *self-actualisation*.

Distortions in the actualising tendency

Once this differentiation exists within a person it is possible to consider how the actualising tendency could become distorted. If self-actualisation is in no way different from the actualising tendency, then the actualising tendency will function uninhibitedly and the person will naturally continue to maintain and enhance themselves as before. But if there is any discrepancy between the two, then one may begin to function at cross-purposes to the other: the greater the discrepancy, the greater the counter-functioning.

Returning to the babies of the experiment that Rogers referred to, at this stage of their development the actualising tendency functions uninhibitedly within them. Through their own organismic valuing process they function in ways that maintain and enhance themselves. They eat the right types of food in the correct quantities in order to keep themselves nicely balanced. Children generally at this stage of development seem to have a clear sense of what they need and do not need, what they like and dislike. A child does not like the experience of hunger unfulfilled and so will eat. A child enjoys a sense of security and so will value being hugged and caressed. A child enjoys new experiences for the simple sense of discovery that comes with them, such as discovering they can reach and feel their toes for the first time (Rogers, 1973). All of these examples show the actualising tendency at work within the child. The child does not like or value pain, though, or loud and unexpected sounds and this is consistent with the notion that the actualising tendency is concerned with the maintenance and development of life, not the sabotage or destruction of it (Rogers, 1980).

As the child begins to develop a sense of self they become aware of their interaction with others and this brings a new type of sensation. Now, in addition to their own internal valuing process they begin to process their experience in relation to external values. The child needs love and places great value on it, to the extent that they are prepared to adapt their behaviour in order to receive it, even if this contradicts their own internal valuing process. Whether or not this is a learned or inherent need is, for Rogers, somewhat irrelevant – what is important is that the child tends to try to elicit love from significant others (usually parents) by behaving in ways that they hope will achieve this outcome.

While this perceived positive value (the feeling of being loved by the significant other) is in accordance with their own internal values, there is little cause for concern as the two experiences are congruent. But problems start where these two experiences are not the same, where they are incongruent. For example, the child enjoys the moment of experiencing the taste of what grown-ups call 'dirt' but is chastised by the mother, who shrieks, 'Get that out of your mouth, it's disgusting'. Or the child wriggles and screams in a desperate attempt to avoid eating the yukky green stuff that his father is convinced will be good for him: 'Come on, eat it up now like a good boy.' The internal valuing process says one thing yet the other individuals, from whom the child needs love, say the opposite. Because the need for love is so strong it often overrides the child's internal valuing process. Thus the child denies himself the pleasurable sensation of the delight and the disgust of the taste of the stuff called dirt; he tries to force down a little bit of that yukky green food that makes him feel sick. He does this in an attempt to win the love or *positive regard*, as Rogers called it, of the other person (Rogers, 1959). Indeed, this need to receive positive regard is so strong that it can potentially become more powerful than the actualising tendency. Thus, although not a motivational drive (the actualising tendency is the only one in Rogers' theoretical system, as mentioned earlier), ultimately it can be the more dominant force.

Conditions of worth

In the two examples just presented, the positive regard on offer could be described as conditional: the other people (the parents) display displeasure in relation to the child's actions – they clearly value one type of behaviour more positively than another. Rogers believes that the result of this over time is for the child to introject these values and adopt them as if they are their own. Thus the child deserts their own valuing system, which has the actualising tendency as its trustworthy base, and takes on the values of others in an attempt to maintain the positive regard they provide. For Rogers, this is the root cause of distortion in the otherwise healthy and life-enhancing development of the person. Once the child's valuing system moves from an internal to an external source they can be described as having acquired *conditions of worth*, as their sense of worth is dependent on how others regard them. The only way for distortion not to occur is if the positive regard offered is unconditional – if the person can 'perceive that of one's self-experiences none can be discriminated by the other individual as more or less worthy of positive regard' (Rogers, 1959: 208). Rogers believes that such a situation does not exist in real life because everyone experiences some conditions of worth. In theory, though, if unconditional positive regard is always experienced, self-actualisation will be congruent with actualisation and the person will exist in a state of continual self-maintenance and enhancement.

The introjection of conditions of worth starts almost as soon as a sense of self emerges but can continue throughout a person's life. Conditions of worth are not just present between the child and their parents (or significant others) during a certain developmental period, a period that some theories of the person suggest defines the type of person that will emerge into adulthood. A person can continue to be affected by the same or different conditions at any stage of their life. In addition, conditions of worth tend to be communicated in an implicit as well as explicit manner, which perhaps makes it more difficult for a person to realise that the process is occurring. The 'bad boy' or 'bad girl' comments that the young child commonly hears are often reworked by the parents as the child grows older, perhaps resulting in 'You should do your homework tonight' or 'I don't want you hanging around with that boy, he's a bad influence on you.' These are still explicit statements of the parents' values in relation to their child's behaviour, even if the child is older now. Often, though, an explicit statement will not be made but the child will still introject the value that they feel is implicit. For example, a daughter is excited about the thought of one day becoming a doctor but her father always changes the subject if she mentions this to him. He does, however, become interested and animated when she talks of helping him out at the weekends at the family's shop, as he has a secret wish that she might become his full-time work colleague and eventually carry on with the family business. Slowly but surely the daughter lets go of her dream of becoming a doctor as she realises that what she really wants is to go into business with her father. Thus she has adapted her thoughts and behaviour in order to comply with the conditions of worth offered by her father.

Of course, both explicit and implicit statements can come from people other than parents: brothers, sisters, aunts, uncles and other members of the extended family may also have an impact, perhaps coming together to represent a collectively held value. A typical example of this is where the teenage son or daughter is the only or first person in the family to go to university. In this situation the value judgements of the family tend to fall into one of two categories: the family is either intensely proud of the child's achievement, or is highly sceptical of the value of higher education. For the child, this can be extremely difficult if, on the one hand, they actually want to give up a university course that they are not enjoying (and endure the family's disappointment) or, on the other, are determined to complete their course and graduate with a good qualification (at the risk of being ostracised by the family).

The complex nature of conditions of worth

The need for love or *acceptance*, as Rogers often described it (1951, 1959, 1980), is experienced not only in relation to the family but also with partners, friends and, in a more ambient sense, through peer groups, religion, culture and society more generally. In the 1960s, Rogers reflected that 'In this fantastically complex culture of today, the patterns we introject as desirable or undesirable come from a variety of sources and are often highly contradictory in their meanings' (Rogers, 1973: 18). Most people would probably agree that our culture at the start of the twenty-first century is even more complex, making it even more difficult for a person to navigate a path of fulfilment and enhancement through this postmodern milieu (see Chapter 8 for further discussion of this).

It is important to consider the effect of such a complex culture on a person's self-concept as this has important implications for how that person develops and changes. The discussion so far has focused on the effect of a single person's value judgement in relation to a single aspect of someone's thought, feeling or action. While such a response representing a singular value or viewpoint can greatly distort a person's internal valuing process, what is equally common is for someone to experience a variety of responses from more than one other person. The result of this type of situation is not such a clear-cut distinction between the internally and externally held value but rather a collage of viewpoints, often contradictory and barbed with paradoxes and catch-22s that create confusion and uncertainty. Rogers (1951) states that:

> The self-structure is an organized configuration of perceptions of the self. … [It is] the organized picture, existing in awareness either as figure or ground, of the self and the self-in-relationship, together with the positive or negative values which are associated with those qualities and relationships, as they are perceived as existing in the past, present, or future. (Rogers, 1951: 501)

Thus, the self is a highly complex gestalt in which elements are constantly shifting from foreground (figure) to background and vice versa, as a result of all the values we experience in all of our relationships throughout our lives. That's quite a few possible permutations!

This notion of a highly complex and sophisticated configuration of self-perceptions has recently been developed by, among others, Cooper (1999), who feels a pluralist conception of self is more likely than a unidimensional one, and by Mearns (1999, 2002) and Mearns and Thorne (2000), where the pluralistic self is conceptualised as 'configurations of self'. As Mearns and Thorne (2000) point out, this is not the same as the seemingly similar state of multiple personality disorder, now called dissociative identity disorder (DID), which describes separate and unrelated characteristics as if they belong to literally different people within the same body. The notion of pluralism in this context is one of several interrelated configurations that are interconnected facets of the self, not separate entities. Some of these configurations could be congruent with the actualising tendency, thus enhancing development, while some might be counterproductive to this process: hence 'growthful' and 'not for growth' configurations (Mearns and Thorne, 2000). Whatever the nature of these configurations, it would seem a more accurate explanation of how the self attempts to adapt to this vast array of ever-changing external values. Of course, at times the configurations may become entangled, perhaps resulting in a highly confusing, disintegrated and destructive self. But it could also be the way in which the self is ultimately able to adapt and overcome the adverse circumstances that have confronted it.

Summary

At the heart of all existing life is the actualising tendency, which maintains and enhances all living beings. As a child develops and grows, a sense of self emerges and a sub-system of the actualising tendency comes into existence: self-actualisation. While this sub-system remains congruent with the actualising tendency there are no major problems, but difficulties arise because the child's internal valuing process gradually becomes influenced by external values. The child needs to receive positive regard or love from external sources such as parents, extended family and friends, so they behave in ways to elicit this love, even though the behaviour may be at variance with their own internal values. Because love is so often given on condition that the child exhibits certain behaviours or views, the child introjects these conditions of worth, thus self-actualising on the basis of values that are conditional and contradictory to its own inherent values – with dysfunctional results. Only if this positive regard (love) is given by others unconditionally can the child remain congruent with its inherent actualising tendency, therefore continuing to develop constructively.

   This view of the person as inherently self-enhancing is crucial to the consideration of how change might occur within the counselling client. At the core of the person-centred therapeutic relationship is a respect for the client's capacity for growth and development. It is not the counsellor as 'expert' who ultimately diagnoses the problem and educates the client in the art of controlling their difficulties; it is the client who, given the right conditions, is able to determine their own ways of resolving problems and of moving forward in a constructive and self-enhancing manner.

Further reading

Rogers, C.R. (1959) 'A Theory of Therapy, Personality, and Interpersonal Relationships, as Developed in the Client-Centered Framework' in S. Koch (ed.), *Psychology: A Study of a Science, Volume 3. Formulations of the Person and the Social Context*. New York: McGraw-Hill, pp. 184–256.
This is Rogers' most detailed description of his complete theoretical system.

Rogers, C.R. (1980) *A Way of Being*. Boston: Houghton Mifflin.
This work offers a more accessible and unsystematic outline of his theory, using less scientific language.

Mearns, D. and Thorne, B. (1999) *Person-Centred Counselling in Action* (2nd edition). London: Sage.
Mearns, D. and Thorne, B. (2000) *Person-Centred Therapy Today: New Frontiers in Theory and Practice*. London: Sage.
Mearns and Thorne (1999) offer a good overview of the person-centred approach and, in their more recent work (Mearns and Thorne, 2000), explore the theory of the self-concept in greater detail with particular reference to what they believe to be its configurational nature.

Bozarth, J.D. and Brodley, B.T. (1991) 'Actualization: A Functional Concept in Client-Centered Psychotherapy: A Statement', *Journal of Social Behaviour and Personality*, 6 (5): 45–59.
In this article Bozarth and Brodley give an in-depth yet succinct commentary on the actualising tendency.

There is an inherent difficulty in the recent trend, particularly within the psycho-medical field, to research counselling outcomes with a view to establishing 'scientifically' whether or not counselling makes people 'better'. Such studies are usually undertaken at the end of an agreed period of counselling or a relatively short time after it has finished. To claim that the outcome of counselling can be determined definitively at any given time is at best optimistic and at worst misleading. Such a claim seems based on the notion that the counselling relationship is analogous to the medical doctor–patient relationship, where medication is prescribed for an illness and the patient is either cured or must try a different treatment. Yalom (2002: 5) remains 'highly sceptical' about the ability to make any kind of accurate, objective assertions about change in relation to counselling. He comments that 'We can observe measurable factors such as weight gain but when it comes to deeper but simpler structures it is so very difficult.' Counselling, it would seem, is not best suited to objective measurable outcomes. Apart from the difficulties of defining and measuring what is meant by change, there is also the important notion that clients do not stop changing when they finish counselling, both in the sense of how they perceive themselves, as well as how they perceive and evaluate the counselling they received (see the reference to Rogers' client, Gloria, in Chapter 1.) Thus, legitimate observations can be made about certain aspects of counselling, such as whether a client feels better (or worse) after a counselling session or series of sessions. But this is different from objectively measuring whether counselling has made a person better or not: this implies that counselling has had its effect, and *all* the effect it can or is likely to have, at a set point in time.

Rogers' theory of change

This leads us on to Rogers' theory of change, which has at its heart the notion that change is an ongoing process. The word 'personality' has been purposely omitted from this chapter's heading in order to reflect this, as in our society it still seems to carry overtones of 'personality type' when used in this context, suggesting that a person is of one type or another and unlikely to change. Rogers' theory of change does not propose a stage-by-stage process from one fixed state to a new and, once again, constant state (although he did loosely demarcate various stages within the process, as will be described). Instead he suggests that the movement that occurs is simply one towards being in a state of change:

> Individuals move, I began to see, not from a fixity or homeostasis through change to a new fixity, though such a process is indeed possible. But much the more significant continuum is from fixity to changingness, from rigid structure to flow, from stasis to process. (Rogers, 1967: 131)

This hypothesis, based on his experience of clients, was something of a surprise to Rogers who had not expected to arrive at such a provocative notion. Indeed, he recognised that some people might feel that this type of change was not a desirable outcome. Even some within the person-centred approach found this concept, with a seeming lack of any coherent identity, difficult to swallow (for example, Van Belle, 1980).

Rogers outlined many of his ideas regarding developmental changes through counselling in 1951, in *Client-Centered Therapy* (particularly in a chapter entitled 'A Theory of Personality and Behaviour') and in his comprehensive 1959 statement of his theoretical system. While these works are highly relevant, they describe some of the more intricate changes that occur within the person and these will be examined in the next chapter. It was not until a little later that he developed a more process-oriented conception of counselling (1967) and this is what will be summarised here. In a sense, this chapter is focusing on *what* happens and the following chapters will go on to examine *how* and *why* it happens.

Rogers' 'process conception of psychotherapy'

Rogers (1967: 125–59) delineates seven stages within a process that exist on a continuum, with stasis or fixity at one end and change or flow at the other. However, he is keen to stress that the number of stages is not crucial as there will always be any number of intermediate points along the continuum. He does believe, though, that it is highly unlikely that a person might live and experience one aspect of their life at one end of the continuum and another aspect of their life at the opposite end of the continuum. A person's characteristics and behaviour overall, he conceptualises, will tend to fall around about the same point on the continuum, even if there is some relatively small differentiation. He also thinks that a person will be unlikely to move from stage two to stage four, say, without going through stage three. Thus he conceptualises these stages in loose terms with much interplay between them along the continuum, as outlined below.

Stage one

It is unlikely that a person at this stage will even come for counselling, as they do not recognise or own their feelings nor any of the meanings that might be attached to those feelings. The person at this stage does not perceive themselves to have any problems; if they were to, these problems would be externalised and not to do with 'self'. In other words, they lack self-awareness. Life is viewed very much in black and white; their interaction with the world is based solely on past experiences that have become rigid benchmarks. Clients at this stage who do come for counselling tend not to come back after the first session as counselling is not seen by them to be helpful or appropriate – the idea of talking about themselves in order to effect change seems pointless.

Stage two

In this stage a person is slightly more able to express their thoughts and feelings, perhaps identifying that they are experiencing some kind of problem. But any such problem is still perceived as being something external to them – there is still no sense of personal ownership and responsibility. Rogers gives the example of a client who, when asked by the counsellor what brought them to counselling, says something like 'the symptom was being depressed'. He reflects that such a client is not saying 'I am depressed': there is no ownership of the problem. The client at this stage would not even say 'I was depressed', although such a statement might be more likely to be given if it is attributed to the past. Thus a person at this stage still has little or no self-ownership and certainly none in relation to their present experiencing. A client's common opening statement of 'the doctor's diagnosed depression' tends to be associated with this stage.

Stage three

Rogers observes that clients are most likely to enter counselling at this stage. There is slightly more awareness of self here, although a true sense of self-ownership still does not exist for the client in relation to their present experiencing. Clients might talk about how they used to feel when they were younger generally, or perhaps in relation to a particular period of time. But in discussing present thoughts and feelings they still tend to externalise them, maybe by relating them to someone else, such as 'I described it the way my dad would do', or 'I'm just like my mum – she does that.' There is a greater expression of feelings than before but such feelings tend to be viewed as wrong and shameful. Benchmarks or *constructs* about the world and the client's experiencing of it still tend to be fairly rigid but there is some awareness at this stage that these are personal constructs and not necessarily facts. Rogers (1967: 136) offers the following example from a client who says: 'I'm so much afraid wherever affection is involved it just means submission. And this I hate, but I seem to equate the two, that if I am going to get affection, then it means that I must give in to what the other person wants to do.' Thus, importantly, at this stage there is also some awareness of contradictions within experienced feelings and meanings.

Stage four

If most clients are likely to enter counselling at stage three, Rogers believes the majority of therapeutic work will be in dealing with stages four and five. At stage four the client still experiences thoughts and feelings from the past, but these are more intense now and there is an increased tendency to experience things in the present, although such experiencing is still often uncomfortable and threatening. Thus there is little acceptance within the client of these experiences. The client is, however, beginning to question the validity of their thoughts and views about the world and there is greater discovery of what constructs the client actually holds. The client is also beginning to be aware of the sense of unease that accompanies their realisation that there are discrepancies between some of these constructs.

Stage five

At this stage there is a genuine embracing of self-ownership and responsibility of thoughts and feelings, with a more critical analysis of the client's own constructs, perhaps leading to a review or change of a held belief. Thus constructs are no longer as rigid as initially conceived as they are now experienced as changeable. For example, a client might comment 'I used to think that, but I'm not so sure any more.' Or even more definitively, 'I used to think that, but I just don't any more – I was wrong, it's not like that … maybe it was true then, but not any more.' Such a comment reflects a recognition that past experiences do not necessarily dictate present ones. It also shows that there is a strong sense of self-experiences being owned, not externalised.

   Such a realisation may seem quite cognitive but another characteristic of this stage is the greater degree of expression of current experiences. Experiences may still feel quite uncomfortable but now there is a preparedness to allow them to flow anyway – to risk the feeling that accompanies them in an open and undefended manner. Continuing the previous example, the client describes a shift in awareness of a particular matter but then goes further by commenting, 'and I feel embarrassed by that … right now I feel such a fool – oh, I'm so stupid! …' and, after a pause, 'Oh, I was so stupid ... but maybe that's OK – everyone makes mistakes, right?' In this example the client allows the flow of experience to occur and it begins to change, not coincidentally, as they begin to explore the idea that perhaps this feeling, and even the change in feeling that seems to be occurring, is acceptable. A key element in the facilitation of this stage is the role played by the counsellor, who has hopefully created a relationship in which the client can openly begin to allow this flow of experience to occur (see Chapters 6 and 7). Indeed, the willingness of the client to express openly how they are feeling in the moment with the counsellor is a key characteristic of this stage or, perhaps more accurately, of the transition from this into the sixth stage.

Stage six

In this stage much of the process that has gone on before in many ways reaches its fruition. Moment-to-moment experiences flow almost completely uninhibitedly, all the time informing and changing the client's sense of self. Constructs based on past experiencing either disappear or are tentatively reformed in relation to these current experiences and are now only held in fluid form. The incongruence between experience and awareness that previously had been perceived as threatening is now embraced and fully perceived. The client explores all aspects of the incongruence which, as a result, dissolves into congruence.

Perhaps for the first time, there is a noticeable physiological accompaniment to the client's experiencing at this stage, such as crying, smiling, audible sighs and posture change. While some of these may have occurred before, they are happening now because of the freedom exuding from the client in their own experiencing of themselves. Rogers comments that it is hard to capture the essence of this stage in words but he attempts to describe it by suggesting that the client is no longer conceptualising a 'problem' as such, whether it be external or internal, but is simply living their experiences in an accepting and thoughtful manner.

Stage seven

In this final stage the client develops all the characteristics of stages five and six a little further. There is a genuine naturalness about all of these aspects now, as the client becomes fully acclimatised to functioning in the ways described. The counsellor's facilitation is now of much less importance as the client is functioning equally well outside of the counselling setting as within it. As Rogers describes:

> The client has now incorporated the quality of motion, of flow, of changingness, into every aspect of his psychological life, and this becomes its outstanding characteristic. He lives in his feelings, knowingly and with basic trust in them

and acceptance of them. The ways in which he construes experience are continually changing as his personal constructs are modified by each new living event. ... He is aware of himself, but not as an object. Rather it is a reflexive awareness, a subjective living in himself in motion. He perceives himself as responsibly related to his problems. Indeed, he feels a fully responsible relationship to his life in all its fluid aspects. (Rogers, 1967: 154–5)

Thus at this stage the client's transformation is complete. At one end of this continuum was a person with little or no self-awareness, with no self-ownership or sense of freedom through change, living removed from their own experiencing in a pre-constructed and rigid world. Now, at the other end of the continuum, they are living a free flowing existence full of richness and vitality, experienced through accurate and ever-changing self-awareness that is being constantly updated. They are finely attuned to themselves and are thus appropriately self-responsible. But what is absolutely crucial for Rogers (1967: 158) is not that the client has gone through these changes and moved along the continuum; it is that they have become 'an integrated process of changingness'.

As suggested earlier Rogers is well aware that, for some, such a psychological state would be far from desirable: a state of ever-changingness might seem too ephemeral to have any kind of tangible meaning or value. However, if it is the high level of self-acceptance in a person that allows them to accurately perceive all their experiences, both past and present, there is a simple implication that they will be forever changing as a result of encountering an unending stream of new and different experiences. Viewed in this way, such a state is no longer an abstract and intangible speculation but a definition of a person liberated from the constraints of self-non-acceptance. Thus the person functioning at stage seven and beyond 'approaches the realisation that he no longer needs to fear what experience may hold, but can welcome it freely as a part of his changing and developing self' (Rogers, 1967: 185).

The fully functioning person

Rogers describes such a person as 'fully-functioning', a concept that he holds as an ideal, believing that very few people are actually able to function in this way. But if such a fully functioning person were living what he calls 'the good life', they would be living a process, as the good life is a direction, not a destination (Rogers, 1967: 186). This good life is characterised by many of the aspects mentioned in relation to stages six and seven of Rogers' process model, but he emphasises openness to experience, existential living, in the sense of living each moment to the full, and a high degree of trust in the person's own organism. He believes that the reason most of us get stuck, why most of us fail to live the good life, is that we attempt to fit our experiences into our constructs and preconceived ideas of what an experience should be, rather than allowing our experiences to inform and guide our living. Thus we are too caught up in trying to include information that is not present or pertinent to a particular current experience to the exclusion of the information that *is*.

Rogers believes there are a number of implications that follow from his observations of what the good life might constitute. These include the hypotheses that a fully functioning person would:

- tend toward being more creative
- be less constrained in their living in the sense of the ubiquitous 'freedom versus determinism' debate
- find a greater richness due to their increased variety and range of experiences
- be increasingly trustworthy and constructive, not just in terms of their development as an individual but also in relation to their functioning with others and within society as a whole. This last point warrants some further discussion as it has increasingly become a matter of contention in recent years.

Pro-social or individuocentric?

As with all schools of thought within counselling, indeed within any system or organised theory of any discipline, the theorist's own background, philosophy, psychology, etc., will have a profound effect on that system of thought. As Jung observes, 'every psychology – my own included – has the character of a subjective confession' (Stevens, 1994: 24). Rogers and person-centred counselling are no different in this respect and the shortcomings for some of person-centred theory is that it is limited in its approach by the personal and cultural influences that permeate Rogers and his writings. It is argued that the theory is a product of its time, representing both the optimism and individualism of post-war America; the latter, when taken to mean a freedom for the individual to do whatever 'feels good', being exemplified by the late 1960s and early 1970s generation. By placing the actualising tendency and the experiencing of the individual at the very centre of his theory, Rogers seems to have invited criticism of the theory as being too individuocentric. At best, the critics state, this limits its relevance and applicability to non-western cultures and, at worst, results in a tendency towards increasingly selfish living as the needs of others are eschewed in favour of the needs of the self.

Criticism has come from within the person-centred community, most notably from Holdstock (1993, 1996a, 1996b) as well as from outside it (for example, Laungani, 1999). Holdstock's concern is that this essentially westernised view of the self emphasises autonomy and independence of the individual. This simply does not fit with non-western cultures, where a sense of self may be located in the family or larger social unit, or even within people's 'relationship with the metaphysical' (Holdstock, 1993: 243). Laungani seems more concerned with how a person from an Indian or Pakistani cultural background could conceive of entering into a counselling relationship which supposedly focuses on promoting the rights of the individual. Given the traditionally hierarchical nature of such an individual's social networks, Laungani therefore believes that counselling would have no meaning or value.

Some female writers (for example, Josselson, 1987) have viewed individuocentric theories of self to be a particularly male phenomenon. Josselson argues that due to early developmental factors, largely to do with the daughter's strong bond with the mother, girls tend to have a much less rigid sense of self than boys and a greater sense of connectedness as opposed to separateness. With this in mind, Holdstock summarises some of the essential differences between how men and women view the self as follows:

> Thus women grow up with a relational sense of self. Identity means 'being with'. ... Unlike males who are brought up in a culture stressing self-assertion, mastery, individual distinction, and separateness ... women are raised in a culture of *communion*, stressing contact, union, co-operation, and being together. (Holdstock, 1993: 235, original italics)

These are fierce criticisms indeed but although Rogers' theory is undoubtedly a product of who he was at that time – a male, white, post-war American – his emphasis on self has not been at the exclusion of the society in which the self exists and interacts. He has been clear throughout his writings (for example, 1951, 1967, 1973) that the self, with the actualising tendency as its trustworthy base, is inherently pro-social. Mearns and Thorne (2000) rightly raise our awareness of the importance of the dialogue that occurs within any individual between the forces of the actualising tendency and those of 'social mediation', which they observe are far too often characterised as 'good' and 'bad' respectively by the person-centred practitioner. Any attempt to facilitate the actualising tendency by effectively pathologising and rejecting societal influences is erroneous: the actualising tendency is pro-social *not* anti-social; one does not exclude the other and should never be thought of as doing so. This fact can get lost when considering the theory, as so often clients are attempting to deal with the conditional messages they have received from society, be it from parents, friends or the wider social context. As Van Kalmthout (1998) reflects, though, the notion of relationship is fundamental to person-centred theory and therapy: the root of a person's problems is conceptualised in interpersonal terms, as is the counselling relationship.

Rogers firmly believes that the need for communion and harmony with others is fundamental to the actualising tendency and therefore to the person, observing that 'We do not need to ask who will socialise him, for one of his own deepest needs is for communication and affiliation with others' (1967: 194). This is not an ethical stance, however; Rogers is not suggesting that people will adopt an altruistic view because of some moral or religious imperative. His argument is straightforward – a person is inherently pro-social. This standpoint may seem at odds with an actualising tendency that wants for nothing but the maintenance and enhancement of the organism. But a fundamental element of that single motivational force is the need to be valued, loved and accepted (positively regarded) by those around one (Tolan, 2001).

Thus in order for such a relationship to occur, a person must develop ways of interacting with those around them that will instigate such a relationship. The fully functioning person, who is free to allow all self-experiences into awareness because there is no need for defence, will similarly feel no need to defend themselves against the threat that others may pose. Such a person will therefore be more likely to be open to the idea of relationships. Given the right conditions, therefore, a person will want communality as opposed to isolation:

> I dare to believe that when the human being is inwardly free to choose whatever he deeply values, he tends to value those objects, experiences and goals which make for his own survival, growth, and development, and for the survival and development of others. I hypothesize that ... in *any* culture, given a climate of respect and freedom in which he is valued as a person, the mature individual would tend to choose and prefer these same value directions. (Rogers, 1973: 26, original italics)

This would seem to answer Holdstock's criticism, mentioned earlier, and Rogers (Kirschenbaum and Henderson, 1990a) and other person-centred writers (Purton, 1998; Thorne, 1991, 2002) have indeed described the metaphysical and spiritual nature of persons and their interaction, as viewed from the person-centred perspective. Perhaps Laungani's concerns are also misplaced. A recent survey (Netto et al., 2001) suggests that clients from an Asian background do indeed value the sense of equality present in the counselling relationship, and that the supposedly individuocentric ethos of counselling models generally would not seem to be a problem. Perhaps it isn't a problem because, at least from the person-centred perspective, the counselling relationship is not attempting to interrupt or impinge upon the client's social existence, but is simply trying to facilitate the client in their exploration of their experiencing.

What all this means in relation to the process of change is that clients will tend to move to a more pro-social rather than individuocentric position as they become more closely attuned to their actualising tendency. As clients become less defensive in the way that they deal with both past and present experiences (as they move through the stages described earlier), they will move toward a more relational existence.

Other person-centred theorists have also conceptualised the change process, one of the most recent being Barrett-Lennard (1998), who delineates five stages in the process of client change. To some degree following Rogers' initial conceptualisation, Barrett-Lennard sees a transformation 'from woundedness to hope' (1998: 110) as being crucial to the process. This transformation is hopefully achieved through two streams of development: the therapeutic relationship and the client's own self-exploration in their search for identity. This is a helpful distinction that is perhaps only implicit in Rogers' model. However, Rogers' description of the process remains the most adept at describing the ongoing nature of the process – it is the constant state of flux that is at the heart of his model; only through this can the self be truly liberated. Various writers (as summarised by Lampropoulos, 2001) have likened the therapeutic process to the development of the nurturing relationship between parent and child. Rogers would have no doubt strongly agreed with this comparison, as long as the nurturing on offer throughout the process was unconditional. By receiving that nurturing, given in an unconditional manner, the child is allowed to develop what is already present – an unconditional nurturing of themselves. The result would be a child – a person – in a continual state of enhancing change and development.

Summary

Rogers' conceptualisation of the process of change is fundamentally simple and yet, even today, remains a radical and provocative statement challenging how we think about clients and ourselves. He outlined seven loosely defined stages that exist on a continuum, along which a client might move prior to, during, and after therapy. The precise demarcation of each stage is of less significance: the essence of his hypothesis is that people move from a rigid and fixed concept of self to one that is in a continual state of change and development. Initially, a client may be unable to allow into their awareness any experiences that do not fit with a set of rigidly held beliefs about the world and the people in it. Gradually though, as the client feels less threatened due to the therapeutic relationship, they begin to examine first past and then present experiences. As the client begins to be aware of these experiences they take ownership of them as they assimilate them into their self-structure, which becomes increasingly flexible and flowing. Ideally, a point is reached at which no experience is too threatening to be allowed into awareness: a self of continual changingness.

Rogers hypothesises that a person in this type of state will be fully functioning, adapting and developing in a continual state of change and growth. Such a person is likely to be creative, experiencing a certain freedom in day-to-day living, as well as being self-enhancing and constructive, as they live and grow with the actualising tendency as their trustworthy motivational force. But, perhaps surprisingly, all this growth is not just focused on self-development; a person naturally also becomes more pro-social and experiences an ever-deepening sense of community and relationship with others. There is an inherent need to develop this type of existence and, once a person no longer perceives their own experiences as threatening, they will be free to allow themselves to cultivate a more communal self.

Thus the person at one end of Rogers' continuum is fundamentally isolated, trapped by their rigid and outdated experiential map and consequently unable to move for fear of disturbing the incongruence they can only barely perceive. At the other end of the continuum, the person is able to embrace that incongruence, which ultimately becomes a part of their ever-changing congruent existence. They flow and develop freely, continually updating their experiential map, no longer afraid. They are free to be themselves – they are free to be themselves in relationship with others.

Further reading

Rogers, C.R. (1967) *On Becoming a Person: A Therapist's View of Psychotherapy.* London: Constable. (First published 1961.)
Rogers offers a detailed description of his conceptualisation of the process of change here, outlining the seven stages of the model and his thoughts on the 'fully functioning person'.

Merry, T. (1999) *Learning and Being in Person-Centred Counselling.* Ross-on-Wye: PCCS Books.
Merry provides a useful summary of both Rogers' and Barrett-Lennard's process models.

The previous chapter described Rogers' overview of the process of change as it occurs within the counselling relationship. The fundamental and radical aspect of his theory is that as a person moves towards a more psychologically healthy state they move towards a state of continual change. Rogers characterised the person in this process as becoming increasingly open to all experiences as they gradually allow into awareness experiences that previously have been either distorted or denied. It is this acceptance of their experiences that ultimately allows change to occur. But how does a person monitor and regulate their experiences and why are some experiences rejected?

Self-concept development

When a baby is born they have no awareness of themselves as a separate entity. As the baby grows older and develops into a child, an aspect of themselves gradually comes to be identified as the self or self-concept (as outlined in Chapter 1). Rogers (1951) suggests that the development of the self-concept starts with a simple awareness of physical experiences and gradually begins to include value judgements in relation to these experiences. The experience of being cold, for example, comes to carry a negative value; the experience of being cuddled is one that comes to be positively valued, etc. Over time, the self-concept becomes an incredibly complex gestalt that consists of all the experiences that are allowed into awareness. Some experiences, though, are not available to awareness, such as fluctuations in blood sugar level and other physiological changes. However, some experiences are available to awareness even though they are not necessarily the focus of attention at a particular point in time. For example, a person's stomach rumbles and it is only then that they realise how hungry they are. Thus there is a difference between experiences that can (but may not) be perceived by the self and those that only register at an organismic level.

Rogers (1959: 199) defines perception as 'a hypothesis or prognosis for action which comes into being in awareness when stimuli impinge on the organism'. He proposes that when something comes into focus in a person's perceptual field they tend to check it against their past experience of that stimulus and make their best guess about what it is. (For example, a person perceives four fingers and a thumb at the end of their arm – from past experience they decide this must be 'a hand'.) Subception, he suggests, is where there is no recognition of a stimulus within awareness but at an organismic level a discrimination is made, even to the extent that the meaning attached to the stimulus is distinguishable. Rogers defined the self-concept as consisting of all experiences (and values and meanings attached) that are available to awareness and are allowed into the self-structure. Mearns and Thorne (2000: 175), however, rightly extend this definition to be all experiences available to awareness including 'edge of awareness material', meaning that the self-concept is not only made up of what is perceived but also that which is subceived. It would seem the only reason why Rogers did not include subceived experience within the concept of self was because of the desire to work with hypotheses that could be clinically and quantitatively tested in keeping with the research trends of the period (Rogers, 1959: 202–3). Yet the concept of self would naturally seem to lend itself to the inclusion of subceived material; hence, Mearns and Thorne's revision.

The processing of experience

Rogers suggests that there are two main categories of experience that are available to awareness: those that are ignored or discarded because they serve no purpose and those that are attended to. Of the experiences that are given attention, some will be allowed into awareness and accurately perceived or *symbolised*, some will be allowed into awareness but only in a distorted form and some will simply be denied access all together. Experiences are allowed into awareness if they meet a need of the self (for example, the sensation of being hungry) or if they reinforce the structure of the self-concept because they are consistent with it. With regard to the latter point Rogers is clear that an experience will not be accurately symbolised in the awareness of the psychologically maladjusted person if it is contradictory to that person's self-concept, regardless of whether the experience is positive or negative. Indeed the rigidity of the self-concept is a characteristic of the client at the lower end of the seven-stage process of change model discussed in the previous chapter. Rogers explains this resistance in terms of inconsistency – the person wants to avoid inconsistency and so rejects experiences that are contradictory to the self-concept. When an experience is perceived as inconsistent with self then the person will feel threatened; if the experience is one that is only subceived it will produce a state of anxiety as the cause of the threat is unclear (Rogers, 1959). In either case the person will defend themselves in order to maintain the current structure of the self.

It is worth considering this notion of consistency for a moment, as Rogers does not fully expand upon why inconsistent experiences are not usually accepted into the self-concept. First, there is a general human fear of the unknown. This is apparent within our society's popular culture, particularly the horror film, which plays upon our fears by presenting us with the 'who is behind the door in the darkened corner?' scenario. Perhaps the horror film is so popular because it provides a contained (approximately two hours) and slightly removed (the audience views the events happening to someone else) setting in which to explore these fears. Second, in terms of our own internal processes, we have what Warner (1996: 137) describes as 'the deep human tendency to want to have a sense of coherence, to resolve discrepancies in one's experience'. She gives the example of a client who explains that she loves her mother and is looking forward to going home to see her. At the same time, though, she might have a sinking feeling in her stomach, an awareness of tears in her eyes or a passing thought about putting her mother into a home. However, if she were to attend more closely to these experiences she might be left feeling more uncomfortable because she does not know where they will lead. They might lead her to having contrary experiences and thoughts to her already existing concept of how she feels and thinks about her mother, which would leave her feeling unsettled. Thus she does not focus on these experiences, placing little or no emphasis on them because of the risk involved. Third, people tend to get caught in the cycle of wanting to elicit positive regard, aligning themselves with what they perceive to be the required behaviour of significant others and sticking with it. Once in this cycle, it is a greater risk to try a new way of being that will potentially receive no positive regard, than to stick with the behaviour that appears to be rewarded with at least some. Thus people get stuck in an often unsatisfactory cycle as experiences that are contrary to their self-concept cannot be accurately symbolised as this might alter their self-concept and therefore their behaviour.

The denial and distortion of experience

In terms of the developing child Rogers (1951) offers a simple yet powerful explanation of how symbolisation and its denial and distortion might occur. One of the first and most important self-experiences that a child has is that their parents love them; they are loved by their parents and it is deeply satisfying and nourishing to experience themselves as lovable. As the child grows they have other experiences, which they evaluate as satisfying or dissatisfying, because at this stage the self-concept is the accurate symbolisation in awareness of their experience. However, the parents react to certain behaviour of the child (for example, when they hit their baby brother) in a way that suggests to the child that their behaviour is wrong or bad and that when they behave in this way the parents' love for them is withdrawn. The devastating implication for the child is that as a result of their behaviour the child is unlovable and will only become lovable once again if they desist in behaving in this way. Thus the child is faced with a dilemma: if they admit to awareness the satisfaction that their behaviour provides it will be inconsistent with their self-concept of being lovable. Usually, in an attempt to resolve this dilemma, the child will either deny the satisfaction they experienced from entering into awareness or they will distort the symbolisation of the experience of their parents' response. As Rogers states:

> The accurate symbolization would be: 'I perceive my parents as experiencing this behavior as unsatisfying to them.' The distorted symbolization, distorted to preserve the threatened concept of self, is 'I perceive this behaviour as unsatisfying.' ... In this way the values which the infant attaches to experience become divorced from his own organismic functioning, and experience is valued in terms of the attitudes held by his parents, or by others who are in intimate association with him. (Rogers, 1951: 500, original italics)

As a result of this the child's self-concept becomes based on distorted symbolisations. Once constructed in this way, the child tends to try and preserve their self-structure by only allowing into awareness material that is similarly distorted, therefore setting the pattern for their maladjusted development. Thus a conditional relationship is established and perpetuated, a relationship Lyward describes as 'contractual living' (Thorne, 2002: 14). In the majority of relationships, Lyward suggests, positive regard or love is only given on a conditional basis and so most of us live our lives under the terms of this unwritten contract. People dare not break the terms of this contract because that would mean the loss of positive regard from others.

An example of inaccurate symbolisation later on in life might be the teenage girl who enjoys drama classes at school but whose parents think that her interest in acting will not provide a sound basis for any future career and is therefore a waste of time. They believe she should focus on sciences – subjects that she is good at and that will provide her with excellent job opportunities in the future. Consequently she decides to take the science route as she can appreciate her parents' point of view and that it is 'best to be sensible'. She makes such a decision because she has acquired conditions of worth – she thinks to herself 'it's good to stick at what you're best at' and 'to make sensible plans for the future'. But these thoughts are not based on her own inherent values, which have been denied or distorted; they are her parents' values and yet she acts upon this sensory information as if it were her own. Perhaps she decides that acting is simply not for her after all (denial) or that it is stupid and is therefore undesirable (distortion). These could, of course, be genuine choices but in this example the girl has not made decisions based upon her internal valuing system – they are the choices of her parents.

The teenage years in a person's life are perhaps the most likely time when they might consciously try to experiment with their concept of self, often resulting in behaviour that is conceptualised as rebellious by parents and society. Rebellious behaviour during this period of life is often concerned with testing out the unconditionality of the positive regard on offer. In other words, the teenager decides it is time to find out whether their parents' love for them really is unconditional or not. In a wider sense, the teenager may also be testing out whether society accepts them for who they are – for the way that they dress, the type of music they like and the values that such attitudes and behaviour represent. Indeed, the teenager *is* rebelling in a sense, as they attempt to explore their concept of self and grapple with the central question of 'Who am I?' This may mean trying out different ways of being to see how they fit against societal norms. Much of this testing out will be about discovering what feels right internally. But so much of it will be governed by conditions of worth – from parents and from friends and peer groups. Thus the searching for self-identity will be done in the context of what is perceived by the teenager to be accepted or rejected by others.

Accurate symbolisation

Returning to the child's dilemma in the earlier example, Rogers suggests that in order to avoid placing the child in this predicament the parent must genuinely accept the feelings of satisfaction the child experiences in relation to the 'wrong' behaviour. In doing so they will be accepting the child as a whole person having a variety of different attributes and not as being simply lovable or unlovable. The parent must also negotiate accepting their own feelings that their child's behaviour is unacceptable. Should they be able to achieve these things the crucial difference would be that the child's concept of self as lovable would not be threatened. Then the child would be free to symbolise accurately both the feelings of satisfaction in relation to this 'wrong' act as well as their perception of their parent's disliking of the behaviour. As their sense of self as lovable is not threatened, the child would be able to consider an appropriate response to the situation with their own internal values as their trustworthy base. Rogers warns this will not necessarily mean that the child immediately acts in a way that is socially desirable or even pleasing to their parents. But considering the pro-social nature of the actualising tendency, the child will ultimately choose constructive actions on a personal and social level if they are allowed to symbolise accurately their experience in this way:

> When the individual perceives and accepts into one consistent and integrated system all his sensory and visceral experiences, then he is necessarily more understanding of others and is more accepting of others as separate individuals. (Rogers, 1951: 520)

Congruence and incongruence

Many person-centred writers have noted the complex nature of Rogers' notion of congruence and several have attempted to clarify exactly what is meant by this multifaceted concept (for example, Brazier, 1993; Haugh, 1988, 2001; Lietaer, 1993; Tengland, 2001; Tudor and Worrall, 1994; Wilkins, 1997). At least some of the confusion would seem to arise as a result of congruence being considered within two different but related contexts, what Brazier (1993) refers to as implicit and explicit congruence. The former is concerned with the *intra*personal (an individual's awareness of their own experience) and the latter, *inter*personal (the communication of congruence between two people, usually therapist and client). The interpersonal setting is relevant to the consideration of the role of the counsellor but of greater interest for this chapter is the individual's congruence between self-concept and organismic experience.

As Tengland (2001) identifies, according to Rogers, incongruence between self-concept and organismic experience is the cause of all psychopathology within an individual and therefore must be able to account for all maladaptive behaviour. Tengland also observes that a 'narrow' interpretation of what is meant by self-concept (i.e. simply a person's view of themselves) could not sufficiently account for all mental health problems. He offers the example of a parent who denies or distorts their experience of realising their son is taking drugs. This might not involve the parent's self-concept in the narrow sense, Tengland argues, as 'the parent might just "want to" protect the conception of the son as well-adjusted' (2001: 162). An argument could be presented, however, that the parent's denial or distortion of this experience *is* in relation to their own self-concept as they may feel their son's drug-taking is an indication of his discontentment, which is in turn a reflection on their parenting skills and thus relating to themselves. Nevertheless, it would seem likely that in order to accommodate all types of situations and problems that occur in life, a broader definition of self-concept is more appropriate, something like 'concept of self in the world'. Incongruence exists, therefore, where a person's self-concept (in the broad sense) is at variance with their organismic experience; experiences cannot be accurately symbolised in awareness and so must be distorted or denied. Change occurs if the person feels fundamentally unconditionally positively regarded (or loved) and so is able to symbolise experiences accurately because they do not pose a threat to their self-concept. For the developing child, this is made possible by the parent if they can embody the qualities discussed earlier, which are very similar to the necessary qualities required of the counsellor for change to occur within the counselling relationship (Biermann-Ratjen, 1996; Warner, 1996). For the client, change occurs if the counsellor can facilitate the client's return to symbolising their experience accurately, as they did before acquiring their conditions of worth. Thus, as Biermann-Ratjen

(1996: 13) emphasises, movement occurs within the client because of 'a change in the *process of evaluating experience*' (original italics).

Acknowledging and exploring incongruence

The process of allowing into awareness organismic experiences that do not fit with the self-concept is often painful and far from straightforward, as the following example illustrates.

> Stephen had experienced a history of conditional worth, particularly in relation to his appearance, as he had been overweight from quite an early age and was bullied by other children at school. Ironically, he had received the message that he was not acceptable from teachers, doctors and nurses too, who had all played a part in organising an almost constant monitoring of his weight and programmes to reduce it. Although this was no doubt in an attempt to improve his situation, the effect was simply to emphasise that it was not all right to be overweight. Over the years he had tried numerous diets as he struggled to conform to people's expectations. None has ever worked in the long run, though, and he has been left despising and fearing everything connected with dieting because of how it makes him feel: frustrated, inadequate and a failure. But now, because his weight is possibly having an adverse effect on his health, he is reluctantly considering going on a diet once again after being advised to do so by his GP. This is producing some conflicting emotions within him. He hates everything that is connected with food – it has brought him so much distress and has such negative connotations – and yet, he is increasingly able to acknowledge that he likes eating food. But his internal value of enjoying eating food does not sit well with the external value imposed on him, which has consistently asserted that liking food is bad because it means putting on weight. Bravely allowing himself to explore his feelings more fully, he acknowledges that going back on a diet would be admitting defeat; specifically, it would mean giving in to the bullies and admitting that they were right – that everyone was right: it is unacceptable to be overweight. Yet as he allows these painful experiences into awareness in their fullness, and to embrace these experiences is excruciatingly painful, he also realises that perhaps he *wants* to try and lose some weight for the sake of his own health. And in that realisation, he acknowledges that his GP is not saying he is unacceptable – the doctor is simply advising him on what is best for his health.

This is by no means the end of the story for Stephen; it is not as if miraculously everything will be fine now that he has made this connection. However, through his acknowledgement and exploration of his incongruence, Stephen has arrived at a more accurate symbolisation of his experiences and therefore is more likely to make decisions about this very difficult matter based on his own internal values rather than on the external influences that have previously governed the process. In acknowledging and exploring his sense of incongruence he has allowed himself to differentiate between past and present constructs. He is able to let go of an old construct – that people punish him for being fat – and recognise that his current doctor is not being in any way malicious. His GP is *not* telling him that he is unacceptable, as Stephen had previously experienced other professionals doing, but is offering to facilitate Stephen's management of his own health.

Allowing contradictory experiences into awareness is unlikely to be easy and will often be confusing as well as painful. In Stephen's case, he is having to negotiate an incongruence between liking food because of the pleasure it brings him and hating food because it makes him put on weight. Putting on weight has led to people viewing him as unacceptable, which in turn has led to a vicious cycle of dieting. He has come to despise everything connected with dieting but is now having to consider going on a diet for his own health. Trying to untangle these interrelationships would be a difficult cognitive task in itself, but when there are highly emotive connotations involved it makes such a process all the more challenging. But it is through this acknowledgement and exploration that change can occur. For as he is able to realise that his GP and perhaps others around him are not saying he is unacceptable, he is increasingly less likely to conceive of himself as being unacceptable. In other words, he is beginning to offer himself unconditional positive self-regard. As he begins to be more self-acceptant, in turn the rigidity of his self-concept will begin to relax, leading to a more fluid and changeable self that is able to assimilate experiences more accurately. Ideally, as for all of us, such self-acceptance ultimately leads to a state of little or no incongruence.

Summary

As soon as a person develops a sense of self this acts as a gateway for all stimuli that impinge upon awareness. Some stimuli, such as certain physiological changes, will never be available to awareness but the self-concept can potentially be affected by all perceived and subceived (edge of awareness) material (Mearns and Thorne, 2000). Not all stimuli will come into focus, though, and much will be ignored as it is of no use or interest to the self-concept. Of the experiences that are of significance, some may be allowed into the self-concept but some may be distorted or even denied access completely. Unless a person is fully functioning (or somewhere near it) their self-concept will feel threatened by any experience that is not consistent with its existing structure, forcing the person to defend themselves against this threat either by distorting it into an acceptable format or by denying the experience completely. Thus experience will be inaccurately symbolised and the misalignment of self-concept and experience will continue and possibly increase. Such a rigid self-concept, formed and shaped by the conditions of worth acquired over time, is unlikely to be capable of change and will remain caught in a cycle of attempting to elicit positive regard.

In order for a person to break free of this cycle they need to be able to accurately symbolise their experiences. Ideally there must be an acceptance of all experiences into awareness in an unadulterated form but usually this would not be achieved with *all* experiences. Indeed, the transition from inaccurate to accurate symbolisation is far from straightforward. But where accurate symbolisation does occur within a person there will no longer be incongruence between self-concept and organism and they will grow and develop in a constructive manner as the actualising tendency will be uninhibited.

Unconditional positive regard from the parent (or significant other) to the child makes accurate symbolisation possible as the child's sense of self as fundamentally lovable is not threatened. Whatever the reaction of the parent might be to certain behaviour, if there is no threat of love being withdrawn the child is free to symbolise the experience accurately and process it at an organismic level. Similarly the counsellor can liberate the client by providing the same quality of relationship, enabling the client to begin to symbolise accurately experiences that previously have been too threatening to allow into awareness. For the client, then, it is the unconditional nature of the positive regard on offer that enables them to re-establish contact with their internal experiencing process. The more the client genuinely experiences this from the relationship, the more fully they can embrace their stream of ever-changing experience without the paralysing trepidation that had previously dominated. The need for the defences of denial or distortion will be no more.

Further reading

Rogers, C.R. (1951) *Client-Centered Therapy: Its Current Practice, Implications and Theory*. London: Constable.
Rogers, C.R. (1959) 'A Theory of Therapy, Personality, and Interpersonal Relationships, as Developed in the Client-centered Framework' in S. Koch (ed.), *Psychology: A Study of a Science, Volume 3. Formulations of the Person and the Social Context*. New York: McGraw-Hill, pp. 184–256.
In both of these works Rogers provides an in-depth description of how the self-concept deals with experience.

Biermann-Ratjen, E.A. (1996) 'On the Way to a Client-Centred Psychopathology', in R. Hutterer, G. Pawlowsky, P.F. Schmid and R. Stipsits (eds), *Client-Centered and Experiential Psychotherapy: A Paradigm in Motion*. Frankfurt am Main: Peter Lang, pp. 11–24.
Biermann-Ratjen outlines the importance of congruence in any client-centred model of psychopathology.

Tengland, P.A. (2001) 'A Conceptual Exploration of Incongruence and Mental Health', in G. Wyatt (ed.), *Rogers' Therapeutic Conditions: Evolution, Theory and Practice. Volume 1: Congruence*. Ross-on-Wye: PCCS Books, pp. 159–73.
Tengland offers a thought-provoking consideration of congruence in the context of a theory of mental health.

In order for constructive change to occur a person has to be able to acknowledge and accept their experiences; only through accurate symbolisation can the self-concept assimilate experiences that may then engender change. A person who is psychologically maladjusted, however, will reject experiences that are inconsistent with self either by denying or distorting them. Such a person will want to maintain their rigid structures of self, as within these there is safety from the uncertainty and threat of inconsistent material. But the self-concept is not usually a unidimensional entity with just one basic construct. It is true that the rigidity of the maladapted self-concept leads to an over-simplification of the world and an individual's experience of it, as described in the lower stages of Rogers' process continuum. More commonly, though, a person develops a complicated network of interrelated constructs over time, leading to an intricate and interrelated three-dimensional self. A person does not simply think of himself as a man, for example, but as a man who is a father, a husband, a librarian (his profession), a film-lover, a football fanatic, etc. In this sense there is more than one aspect or quality that goes to make up the man's concept of self. For instance, what goes to make up his concept of self as a father? Does he think of himself as a good and loving father, or a fun father who is spontaneous, or one that is dull and perhaps a disappointment to his children, or a reluctant father who struggles to come to terms with parenthood? To complicate matters still further, his view of himself as a father may be a combination of these conceptions of self, not just one or another. Bearing in mind Rogers' statement that experiences will be rejected that are inconsistent with self, it is clear that the evaluation of experience is far from straightforward. There is not a simple 'yes' or 'no' answer to the question 'Is this experience consistent with my self-concept?' because the experience could fit with some aspects of self but not others. The evaluation of experience, therefore, is a fantastically complex process. Various theorists have presented ways of conceptualising the self and it will be useful to consider some of these here; an awareness of how the self-concept might be constructed will no doubt aid the counsellor in their attempt to facilitate change.

Configurations of self

Rogers describes the self-concept as follows:

> The self-structure is an organised configuration of perceptions of the self. ...It is composed of such elements as the perceptions of one's characteristics and abilities; the percepts and concepts of the self in relation to others and to the environment; the value qualities which are perceived as associated with experiences and objects; and the goals and ideals which are perceived as having positive or negative valence. (Rogers, 1951: 501)

Thus there are a number of self-perceptions within a person that are concerned with how a person views themself, their goals, their interaction with others and the values they place upon their experiences in all of these different contexts. Many clients refer to these different facets of self simply as 'parts' ('there's a part of me that ...') but, as Mearns and Thorne (2000) observe, the term 'configuration' would seem more apt as these parts do themselves consist of many different aspects and attributes. Keil (1996) conceptualises the self as consisting of 'inner persons', which is also an attempt to capture the flavour of a configurational self-concept. The inner persons have their own individual characteristics but there is also a strong interrelational nature between all of these inner persons, leading to a highly complex and not altogether harmonious self. Mearns and Thorne (2000), building on the work of Mearns (1999), offer the following 'working definition' for the notion of configurations:

> A 'configuration' is a hypothetical construct denoting a coherent pattern of feelings, thoughts and preferred behavioural responses symbolised or pre-symbolised by the person as reflective of a dimension of existence within the Self. (Mearns and Thorne, 2000: 102)

A couple of important elements exist within this statement: first, the notion of a configuration is indeed a hypothetical construct and so cannot actually be directly observed, only hypothesised; and second, the description of the material being 'symbolised or pre-symbolised' makes clear that the material could be already in awareness or at a point where it has not yet entered awareness. These are important factors when considering how the counsellor works with a client in order to best facilitate change. It is essential that the counsellor tracks the client's description of these configurations as it is only the client who can describe the complex and changing nature of their self-concept as *they* understand it. The counsellor must attempt to work with all of these configurations as the client presents them, even though some may be 'not for growth' and therefore supposedly less worthy of the counsellor's positive regard. For change to occur, the client must be able to begin to examine some of the more threatening aspects of a configuration or even a whole configuration itself, which can only happen if the therapist has successfully communicated an unconditional positive regard toward all aspects of the client.

The notion of a configurational self also offers the opportunity for rethinking the process of denial. It is no longer the case that experiences have to be denied if they cannot be symbolised accurately, as there is now the possibility that any inconsistent material can be subsumed within one or other part of the self-structure (Cooper, 1999). Rogers is perhaps suggesting this with his notion of distortion, although he does not overtly describe that the distortion occurs through the manipulation of configurations. Cooper (1999), however, makes the distinction that such experiences are accepted into the self but in such a way as to be consistent with one or other aspect of a configuration. Thus the experience itself is not distorted, as such, but the configuration is manipulated in order to accommodate the experience.

Rice (1974, 1984) conceptualises the self slightly differently, describing categories of experience in terms of 'schemes' (1974) or 'self-schemas' (1984). These terms essentially refer to how a person processes their self-experiences on a cognitive and affective level. Rice suggests that, ironically, schemes are a product of a person's mental agility in processing complex data efficiently. The data relating to self-experiences are extremely complex and, in order to manage that data efficiently, information must be grouped together into similar units. If the experiences are processed in a relatively balanced manner, so that grouping occurs without loss of accuracy, then the schemes will be adaptive. But where there is oversimplification and inaccurate processing such schemes will be maladaptive. In addition, echoing Rogers' notion of self-concept resistance to inconsistencies, Rice observes that once self-schemas are established they are very resistant to information that does not fit with their existing structure. Rice believes that in order for a person to address maladaptive self-schemas there has to be a reprocessing of the cognitive-affective data; this is the task that confronts the client and therapist.

Affective configurations of self

A different conceptualisation of how configurations of self might be constructed is one that groups together experiences in relation to our emotions, such as anger, happiness, shame, sadness, guilt, fear, etc. Such groupings might come about within a person due to a particular event (or series of events) but mainly because of the way in which positive regard is offered to them by their significant others. The result is a rigid configuration that will be resistant to experiences that are contradictory to the existing structure, although one or more configurations may provide a useful vehicle for the distortion of other material. Some examples will clarify how this might occur:

Amjid's life has been influenced by some tragic events. His mum died when he was 14 after a long illness; his best friend was killed in a car crash three years later; now his uncle has been diagnosed with a similar illness to his mum. Amjid is struggling with seeing a point to living, for he is left wondering what is the use in bothering when life is so fragile and can be taken away at any time? His self-configuration, as it currently exists, will be shaped by his sense of apathy: apathy is the defining emotion of his self-concept as it is currently configured. Other experiences, perhaps the enjoyment of going out on his 18th birthday, cannot be accurately symbolised and are subsumed within some variant of the apathy configuration, being redefined as simply confirming the pointlessness of life. Amjid cannot accept into his awareness his enjoyable experience of having a good night out with some friends and instead distorts it, believing such an experience to be ultimately meaningless because it can be snatched away at any moment. This is just what his dad believes – 'what's the point in enjoying yourself when you know it might end at any moment?' This is something he's said to Amjid many times.

Samantha's family are always telling her that she is stupid. When she was younger her sisters teased her because she could never get the dance routines right they practised in their bedrooms. Her dad told her that her failure to get more than two GCSEs was no surprise – he didn't expect her to do well. Her mum is forever telling her that if only she had some common sense she would be getting somewhere in the world by now. Her grandmother chastises her for not being as clever as her cousin Jenny; if only she had done better at school, like Jenny did, she could be working for a good company, like Jenny is. 'Jenny is going places', her grandmother tells her. Samantha's current self-configuration is characterised by her low positive self-regard: she feels worthless. Sometimes the configuration shifts so that a deep sense of shame pervades her sense of self. At other times it is characterised by a feeling of inadequacy. However, against all the odds Samantha is now studying part-time at university after doing an access course and is in her second year. She even got a First (the highest grade possible) in one of her end of year exams but is convinced this is because 'they make the first year easy so you don't get put off – everyone did well in those exams.' The other day her friend told her that she thought Samantha was the brightest person on their course; Samantha dismissed this as ridiculous, deciding that her friend couldn't possibly know because she doesn't take the same course options as her.

Robert comes from what he describes as 'a very traditional family'. His dad's an electrician and has worked from Monday to Saturday every week for as long as Robert can remember. His mum stayed at home and brought up him and his sister but has just got a part-time job at the local supermarket, working three evenings a week. Until last year, when he went to France on tour with the local orchestra he plays in, Robert had never been abroad, as every summer the family would go to Devon for their family holiday. Throughout his life his parents have discouraged him from doing anything that they didn't agree with. As far as Robert is concerned this was basically because the things he wanted to do were different from what his parents had done themselves as they were growing up. Robert is aware that he's increasingly angry about this – it's his life not theirs. But there is something else. He's noticed recently that he's started to turn down opportunities, he's started to always go with the 'safe' option, he's started to say 'no' a lot. He thinks he might actually be afraid: afraid to do what *he* wants. Fear has become the defining factor. Just last week his friend asked him to come backpacking in Australia in the summer. He found himself saying to his friend that he thought he'd better work in the summer instead in order to get down his overdraft – his mum has got him a job at the supermarket.

These examples demonstrate how the self may become configured in terms of emotional states. Amjid's current configuration of self is dominated by apathy. His apathetic state has become rigid and resists new and contrary experience, such as the enjoyment of celebrating with friends because this does not fit with 'what's the point?', an attitude that his father is constantly emphasising. Samantha's configuration is biased towards her sense of worthlessness, which sometimes tends towards a sense of shame, sometimes more towards a sense of inadequacy. She has developed this configuration due to her family's consistent failure to demonstrate to her anything approaching unconditional positive regard. Her concept of self as worthless has developed out of her family regarding her as 'stupid' and is now so inflexible that contrary experiences, such as receiving good grades for essays or praise from a friend, cannot be assimilated into her 'worthless' self. Robert's configuration is dominated by fear – fear of what he wants in life as this might be different from what his parents wanted for themselves. He is also aware of feeling angry but this is currently in the background. His fear prevents him from taking up the opportunity of travelling to Australia – such an act would not fit with his 'afraid' configuration. He can allow himself to work at home during the summer, however, as this is compatible with his current configuration.

   These examples cannot represent all the possibilities of how configurations might be formed in relation to a self-as-emotion configurational model but they can convey the way in which configurations might be constructed in this way over time. An affective configurational model would seem a useful hypothesis to adopt, given the frequency with which clients talk about themselves in terms of their emotional personas. For example, a client, Sonja, talks about 'angry Sonja' during her counselling sessions; 'angry Sonja' is how most people view her but she knows there is a 'hurt, sensitive Sonja' that she hides from everyone. It should be stressed, though, that such a hypothesis is exactly that – a hypothesis. An affective configurational model is not presented here as objective fact; hopefully its worth is in providing an alternative conceptualisation of configurations, thus enabling the counsellor to empathise more accurately with the client as *the client* tries to explore and understand their concept of self. It is only through the client accurately allowing such material into their awareness that change can ultimately occur.

The regard complex

Rogers (1959) proposes Standal's (1954) notion of a 'regard complex'. The regard complex refers to all experiences (and the interrelationship between experiences) that a person discriminates as being related to the positive regard received from a particular social other. This would most obviously be thought of in relation to a single other person, such as a parent, but could equally apply to a group of people or society more generally, perhaps through the role of the media in particular. Rogers hypothesises that if a person receives positive regard from their parent (or social other) in relation to a specific behaviour, this tends to strengthen the whole pattern or *complex* of positive regard that has been previously experienced as coming from that parent. Similarly, negative regard that is received in relation to a specific behaviour will tend to weaken the whole complex of positive regard as previously experienced from that person.

How this actually works in practice will depend on a few variables. Has the positive regard that has been previously received from this person been consistently positive? Has it been sometimes positive but sometimes negative? Has it been quite positive or extremely positive? How many previous experiences are available to draw upon in relation to this particular person's positive regard? What is the time frame in which these previous experiences occurred? With these variables in mind the effect of the other's response on a person's regard complex will largely be determined by the experiences that have preceded their latest experience. For example, a parental response of negative regard toward a specific instance will only slightly weaken the overall complex where previous experiences have been consistently and extremely positively regarded, particularly if this has occurred over a long period of time. In this case, in fact, it would almost imperceptibly dent the regard complex as it would seem insignificant given the previous emphatically positive experiences. Where previous experiences have been far more inconsistent or even negatively biased, however, the scales begin to tip all too easily into an overall complex of negative regard. And where previous experiences have been consistently and extremely negatively regarded over a substantial time period, this will result in an extremely rigid complex of negative regard in relation to the parent. Counsellors working with clients finding themselves in this latter situation may experience the client as almost unreachable, such is the ingrained nature of their negative regard complex in relation to the person concerned. Depending on the importance ascribed to this particular person, this may mean an even more entrenched and inflexible complex. Thus the regard complex can be described as being a function of consistency, duration, level of positive regard and the significance of the social other.

An overarching regard matrix

The notion of the regard complex can be extended into an overarching *regard matrix*, which concerns all self-experiences that relate to positive regard from *all* social others. This offers a more complete conceptualisation of how a person struggles to experience positive regard toward themselves, as usually an individual is influenced by the variables mentioned earlier but not solely in relation to one other person. Parents, carers, siblings, friends, peer groups and societal standards and norms all contribute to make up the regard matrix, which will determine the overall level of positive self-regard. Although the framework for the matrix will be broadly similar for everyone, each person's matrix will be different due to the unique nature of everyone's experience, as the following examples illustrate:

> Ever since she was a child Janet has felt utterly loved by her parents who have consistently supported and encouraged her in just about every activity she has undertaken. Her elder brother has also been a source of great support to her, looking out for her (his kid sister) and yet respecting that she is going to make different choices from him and do her own thing. Her parents divorced when she was eleven, her mum marrying her step-dad a few years later, with whom she also has a very positive relationship. There was a period in school when a group of other kids ganged up on her and made her life 'hell', but through her own determination she managed to move away from that situation within about six months. Now in the final year of her degree course, Janet is considering which job option to take up after being offered two prestigious graduate fast-track appointments.

> David remembers his childhood as being mostly happy. His mum and dad always seemed to be there for him, giving him all the toys, holidays and fun times out he could need. But not long after his ninth birthday his dad started working away from home for long periods and he saw him less and less. During this same period his mum went through a very difficult time; sometimes it felt like she could still be there for him, being attentive and encouraging about what was going on in his school life, but at other times he felt she kept a distance from him, like she wasn't really aware of him and his needs. After leaving home in his late teens, David worked in various countries before returning to live not far from where he grew up. He has been married twice, both marriages ending acrimoniously but for different reasons, leaving him confused as to why they had gone wrong. He has won numerous design awards and is highly respected within his field of work, running a successful company of which he is joint director. He sees his parents fairly regularly now, as they live close by, but his relationship with his dad remains disappointingly distant. His dad has never expressed any pride in his son's success in the design field.

> Clare's life has been characterised by violence. Her dad systematically physically abused her while she was growing up and when he wasn't abusing

her, he was beating up her mum. After years of putting up with this, her mum finally left her dad; Clare didn't see her mum for six months and was subsequently put into care, being placed with a foster family. These were the best two years of her life as at last she felt like she belonged: someone actually wanted her to be around. Due to a variety of complications, however, she was forced to move from that family and go and live in another part of the country. She now finds herself on the periphery of a group of people she's met through the local night-club scene, drifting from one temporary job to another and feeling isolated and disenchanted.

In these examples it can be seen how the regard matrix will be different for different individuals. Janet will no doubt have a high level of positive self-regard due to her regard matrix. Her biological parents have consistently highly valued her over a long period of time, as has her brother, offering her unconditional positive regard. Her more recent relationship with her stepfather has offered her further positive regard and she will also feel valued by society with good job prospects on offer. Her experience of negative regard from some other kids at school was relatively brief so, although it had a negative effect on her, it will not have diminished her self-regard by any great amount. Overall, therefore, her regard matrix consists of mostly very positive experiences, which provide her with a high level of largely unconditional positive self-regard.

The experiences that go to make up David's regard matrix, however, are not so strongly positively biased. While he received consistent positive regard from his parents when he was a child, this has not been sustained into adulthood. From the age of nine through his teenage years, his father was not around to offer any positive regard and his mother was much more inconsistent in what she was able to offer. As an adult, two failed marriages that have ended acrimoniously suggest experiences of ultimately negative regard towards him, from two different and significant people. He has been successful in his career though, receiving a high level of positive regard from within his field of work. But although his relationship with his mum may be better again now, he still receives little or no positive regard from his dad. Thus, overall, his regard matrix consists of mixed experiences and his own level of positive self-regard is likely to reflect this, being of a variable level and mostly conditional.

In contrast, Clare's regard matrix consists of predominantly negative experiences. She consistently received negative regard from her father during childhood and ultimately received no positive regard at all from either parent once she no longer had any contact with them. She had a period of two years where she received consistent positive regard from her foster family but that was only for a limited period and so had only limited effect. She does not currently receive any consistent positive regard from her family unit, friends or peers, or society more generally. Her own level of positive self-regard therefore, conditional or unconditional, is likely to be very low.

These examples cannot begin to cover every possible matrix permutation but they can serve to demonstrate the nature of how regard matrices might be formed. Given the importance of positive regard within person-centred theory it is likely that the regard matrix will influence and affect all other self-concept configurations, as the pre-eminent need of the self is to receive positive regard. Configurations can certainly become distorted due to a person's conditional development, creating some unhelpful and perverse configurations. But all configurations will tend to be influenced by this overarching regard matrix that is shaped and changed by experiences relating to receiving positive regard. Once again, the usefulness of this conceptualisation is in facilitating the counsellor as they attempt to create an environment in which the client can explore all aspects of self. A model of the self-concept can be laid to one side by the counsellor when engaged in a therapeutic relationship but such a model may be useful to the counsellor as they attempt to respond sensitively to any aspect of self the client may chose to share and explore. Given that the self can be so complex, a model may prove useful as a rough outline of what might be occurring. It is essential, of course, that it remains a rough outline that can be flexible and changed depending on the detail. Rogers' (1951: 144) statement in relation to the client is, in this context, just as relevant for the counsellor: 'the map is not the territory.'

Summary

The self-concept is an extremely complex structure that is most likely to be of an interrelated three-dimensional design rather than one that is unidimensional. A few models of the self have been explored here, particularly the notion of configurations as described by Rogers (1951, 1959) and developed by Mearns and Thorne (2000). Configuration is a useful term because it captures the sense that a person's self-perceptions have their own unique attributes and complexities as well as interrelating with each other to produce an overall effect. An alternative configurational model is one that considers the self in terms of our emotions and this is offered as another possibility of how a person might configure their self-experiences. Rogers (1959) also proposes Standal's (1954) theory of a regard complex, which conceptualises the interrelational nature of a person's experiences of positive regard with respect to a significant social other. This regard complex can be described as being a function of consistency, duration, level of positive regard and the significance of the social other, as these are the variables that may affect it. It is suggested that an overarching regard matrix, relating to all positive regard experiences with respect to all significant social others, will permeate all configurations of self at some level.
    Whatever the nature of the model, though, the important element in relation to change is that the client is able to explore, re-examine, confront

and ultimately rework configurations that have been formed through a misrepresentation of their experiences. For change to occur within a client they must be able to symbolise their self-experiences accurately. Most clients, however, have relatively rigid structures that have developed over time into a complex network of configurations within the self. These configurations often take on a life of their own, distorting and manipulating experiences without the client even being aware that this is occurring. Indeed, the labyrinthine nature of the self can be as beguiling to the counsellor as it is to clients themselves. That is why a theoretical understanding of the self-concept might be useful to the counsellor; these different interpretations of the configurational nature of self represent different ways of understanding how the pieces might fit together and interact.

Further reading

Rogers, C.R. (1951) *Client-Centered Therapy: Its Current Practice, Implications and Theory*. London: Constable.
Rogers, C.R. (1959) 'A Theory of Therapy, Personality, and Interpersonal Relationships, as Developed in the Client-Centered Framework', in S. Koch (ed.), *Psychology: A Study of a Science, Volume 3. Formulations of the Person and the Social Context*. New York: McGraw-Hill, pp. 184–256.
Once again these works provide a good starting place as they describe some of the fundamental aspects of the configurational nature of self.

Mearns, D. and Thorne, B. (2000) *Person-Centred Therapy Today: New Frontiers in Theory and Practice*. London: Sage.
Mearns and Thorne extend the notion of configurations and through some edifying examples demonstrate how the complexities of the self-concept can be explored within the counselling relationship.

It is clear from the previous chapters that the accurate symbolisation of experience is crucial to a person's constructive development and functioning. An inability to symbolise experience accurately leads to a distorted and rigid self-concept that is unable to change in response to new and different experiences. But how do experiences and their accurate symbolisation lead to a person being able to function more effectively? How does simply experiencing something lead to change and growth? To put it more crudely, and to paraphrase the observation of many an incredulous client and trainee counsellor, 'How is experiencing my feelings of hurt and sadness *possibly* going to make me feel better?!'

To be that self which one truly is

In arguing that change occurs when people are able to experience themselves more fully, Rogers adopts Kierkegaard's statement of endeavour 'to be that self which one truly is' (Kierkegaard, 1941), as for Rogers it captures the essence of what his clients seem to be aiming for as they struggle in their lives (Rogers, 1967: 166). The important aspect for Rogers is 'being' oneself more fully – an openness to oneself and one's experiences leads to more accurate symbolisation, which in turn facilitates change. Rogers is clearly influenced in his thoughts on 'being' by the writings of Lao-Tzu, the Chinese sage who is thought to have been a contemporary of Confucius. Central to the philosophy of Lao-Tzu is the notion of 'nonaction'. Rather than meaning 'not doing', as might be expected, 'nonaction' is concerned with 'being' – a subtle but important shift in emphasis. Mitchell (2002) describes exactly what underpins this notion of 'non-action' through reference to chapter 48 of the *Tao Te Ching*, a collection of philosophical writings generally attributed to Lao-Tzu:

> The misperception may arise from his [Lao-Tzu's] insistence on *wei wu wei*, literally 'doing-not-doing', which has been seen as passivity. Nothing could be further from the truth. A good athlete can enter a state of body-awareness in which the right stroke or the right movement happens by itself, effortlessly, without any interference of the conscious will. This is a paradigm for non-action:

the purest and most effective form of action. The game plays the game; the poem writes the poem; we can't tell the dancer from the dance.

> Less and less do you need to force things,
> until finally you arrive at non-action.
> When nothing is done,
> nothing is left undone.

Nothing is done because the doer has wholeheartedly vanished into the deed; the fuel has been completely transformed into flame. This 'nothing' is, in fact, everything. (Mitchell, 2002: vii–viii)

Thus if a person can be at one with their actions, the actions no longer involve a sense of 'doing' but simply of 'being'. Such a state of complete synchronisation between person and action results in a unification – a harmonious confluence that transcends the causal process normally involved in an action. In other words, there is no conscious focusing of attention in order to generate the action: the person simply *is* the action.

Indwelling

Following on in this theme, and returning to more modern philosophical writings, Polanyi (1958) uses the term 'indwell' to describe a sense of oneness with knowledge. He rejects the traditional value of scientific detachment as being the most fruitful approach to learning and suggests that an immersion into – a merging with – the subject matter itself is what is actually required. Thus the mathematician dwells in 'the domain of established mathematics ... by losing himself in the contemplation of its greatness' (1958: 195), and a true appreciation of music and the dramatic arts is only achieved if a person is able to 'surrender' themselves to the works of art. Polanyi adds: 'This is neither to observe nor to handle them, but to live in them' (1958: 196). This is the crucial difference for him – being *in* the experience as opposed to observing and analysing it. These latter qualities are important but can only be truly useful if utilised in addition to the experiencing itself, because 'as observers or manipulators of experience we are guided *by* experience and pass *through* experience without experiencing it *in itself*' (1958: 197, original italics). Bohart (1996: 199) seems to be describing a similar relationship when he states: 'Conceptual knowing, thinking, believing, forming concepts, and the like, all come from experiential knowing, and is an attempt to formulate that knowing in words and concepts.' Indeed, Bohart (1996) suggests (and demonstrates) that an actor learning a dramatic role exemplifies why an experiential knowing is of more value: an actor only really 'becomes' the part when they have managed to shift their learning from the intellectual/conceptual to the gut level.

Polanyi describes the framework by which we observe and manipulate experience as a screen that prevents us from experiencing the matter in question. The only way of penetrating the screen is by contemplation:

> Contemplation dissolves the screen, stops our movement through experience and pours us straight into experience; we cease to handle things and become immersed in them. Contemplation has no ulterior intention or ulterior meaning; in it we cease to deal with things and become absorbed in the inherent quality of our experience, for its own sake. (Polanyi, 1958: 197)

There is a strong resemblance here to Rogers' description of empathy, where the focus is on entering the client's frame of reference: both describe an attempt to reach a profound experiential understanding that is made all the more possible by the absence of any value judgement. Indeed, this dual application of indwelling is central to person-centred theory and practice, as elegantly summarised by Sims (1989): 'As clients in psychotherapy, the framework we are trying to dwell in and make useful is ourselves. As psychotherapists in psychotherapy, the framework we are trying to dwell in is the client.'

Thus the emphasis in person-centred counselling is always to facilitate clients indwelling themselves – to create an environment in which clients feel safe enough to try to know themselves. Other therapeutic approaches could be said to indwell the theoretical or action framework that they try to impose on their clients, whereas person-centred therapy attempts to indwell *the client* (Sims, 1989); the counsellor is simply a co-investigator, a research assistant *to* the client (O'Hara, 1986). This emphasis on the client experiencing themselves is clear within Rogers' seven-stage process model (as described in Chapter 2) but how does this 'being', this indwelling, actually bring about change within the person?

As the client gradually feels more trusting of the counsellor and of their relationship they will begin to explore aspects of themselves that previously have been outside of their focus of attention. Such experiencing could take the form of a feeling, an idea or thought, a memory of an event, etc. (O'Hara, 1986). As the client and counsellor attempt to indwell that experience, different aspects of the experience will become apparent to the client. The client then investigates these nuances further, deciding which are most true or relevant for themselves. This may involve a consolidation of an already existing feeling or view, or it may involve the introduction of a new element to the existing self-structure that will therefore require integration. Crucial in this process, indeed what the client is actually striving towards, is the exact (or as close as the client can understand) meaning of their experience (Sims, 1989). It is the personal meaning for the client that will be the building block for change. As discussed previously, the important factor is not what the experience might mean to the therapist or any external observer (for which there might be as many different meanings as observers) but *what the experience means to the client.*

The counsellor may assist this process by offering their observations of what is occurring but only because this enriches the client's construction of their own meaning.

Focusing

Gendlin (1981, 1996) developed a particular method in order to indwell experience, a method that would in turn help to clarify meaning for the client. He called this method *focusing*. Although Gendlin's focusing technique is considered to belong to a particular type of person-centred counselling, namely *experiential* (Sanders, 2000), the process involved exemplifies how change occurs from a more general person-centred perspective and so is worthy of discussion here. Gendlin (1981: 10) describes focusing as follows: 'It is a process in which you make contact with a special kind of internal bodily awareness. I call this awareness a *felt sense*.' A felt sense is a bodily sensation but is not simply a physical sensation like a tickle or a pain; it 'is the body's sense of a particular problem or situation' (1981: 10, original italics). Thus for Gendlin the process of change is concerned with trusting bodily felt senses to guide a person to whatever the problem or concern might be. It is trusting in the wisdom of the body as the body can sometimes appreciate meanings that the mind cannot yet understand; a felt sense is different from an emotion because it will not be something easily recognisable like anger, happiness, sadness, etc., but will be vague and unclear though distinctly perceptible. The process of focusing, in what Gendlin refers to as the Short Form (1981: 173), can be paraphrased as follows:

1 **Clear a space**
  How are you feeling? Don't worry about anything definite – just allow whatever sense comes into your body to answer.

2 **Felt Sense**
  Choose one problem that arises to focus on. Don't go into that problem too much but ask yourself what your body senses when you recall everything to do with that problem.

3 **Get a handle**
  What is the quality of the felt sense – what word, phrase or image would fit it best?

4 **Resonate**
  Try out the word, phrase or image several times to make sure it really fits. If it changes while you are doing this, go with it until it finally fits. Once you've got it, just let yourself feel what it is like for a few minutes.

5 **Ask**
'What is it about this whole problem that makes me feel so ...?' If you get stuck, ask yourself: 'What is the worst aspect of this feeling?' or 'What does this feeling seem to need?'

6 **Receive**
Welcome what came up within yourself. It is only one step on this problem, not the last. Now you've experienced this you can always come back to it later if you want to. (Paraphrased from Gendlin, 1981: 173–4)

The following example, offered by Gendlin (1981: 11–16), demonstrates how this process occurs in practice. A client of his, Fay, telephones him saying that life is too much and that she cannot see the point in living. (A few years earlier she had broken up with a man called Ted whom she really loved. Since then she had been in a string of relationships, unable to re-create the love she had experienced with Ted.) Gendlin asks her what feels so bad. She tells him that she has missed her period and is worried she is pregnant after sleeping with a man named Ralph. 'I miss Ted so much!' she exclaims. 'What if I'm pregnant? Oh God, what's going to happen to me?' At this point Gendlin begins the focusing movements, first asking her to clear a space and then, metaphorically speaking, to stack all of her problems as she currently perceives them in front of herself. After inviting her to consider each one of these problems in turn she identifies two that seem worse than the others: that she misses Ted and that she fears she might be pregnant. When asked which one of these feels worse she says the former and begins to cry, speaking of loneliness and hopelessness.

Now Gendlin invites her 'to go down inside there and see what the worst of that is ... Get to the unclear body sense of all of it.' As she has used focusing before and understands what Gendlin is asking, she gets to a felt sense and then tries to fit a handle to it, responding 'It's all about anger, or something, I don't know ... it's like I'm angry at – why would I be angry?' Here, Gendlin does not offer Fay an analysis of this statement but simply asks her to 'ask the felt sense.' After careful consideration and a clearly audible sigh, she says, 'I'm angry at myself. That's what it is. For sleeping with all those men I didn't love, didn't feel anything for.' After further contemplation she continues, 'And part of it is I'm angry with myself for sleeping with Ralph, maybe getting myself in trouble – an abortion, maybe. And I call myself bad, also, sleeping with a man I don't care for.' Her statement 'And I call myself bad' seems to be a shift. A new element has entered her thoughts now and she continues 'There's a kind of heavy discouraged feeling.' After a further pause, she clarifies what this feeling is connected with: 'It's about all these men I don't care for. I have no sexual feelings for them. ...' However, it seems this still does not capture exactly what she means and she says the word 'discouraged' to herself a few times as she mulls it over. Suddenly, and with great relief, she exclaims 'Weary! That's it. I'm weary. I feel like I'll spend the rest of my life going from one dull man to another, never feeling sexual but never letting myself stop trying. I can see all those men lined up ahead of me, all those blank faces, rows and rows of them from here to the end of my life. I'm condemned not to have sexual feelings, that's what.' Gendlin pauses at this point, wondering if she wants to go into this in more detail but she simply says, 'I feel better now. What a load to get rid of!'

Gendlin summarises Fay's process in this episode as follows:

> *She had changed inside.*
> It had seemed a problem of loneliness. With the first shift it was her anger at herself, and with the next shift it was her calling herself bad. Then the heavy discouragement came up, and with a bodily release it turned out to be a conviction that she would never again have sexual feelings. Even as she sensed this last, it changed in her body. (Gendlin, 1981: 15, original italics)

Thus by focusing on her felt sense and trusting her body she had managed to get to the heart of what was troubling her and had experienced a shift in her feelings about the situation. As Gendlin acknowledges, this might be one shift of many regarding this particular issue but Fay felt better as a result of this process.

There are many similarities between this process using focusing and the counselling process proposed by Rogers, who does not believe such a technique to be required for change to occur. Common to both is the importance of experience and the belief that the client will be able to determine the exact quality of the experience and what it means for them, which will then lead to a shift in feeling and thought. It is this belief in the client's ability to determine what experience means to them that is the defining factor of the person-centred approach and why change occurs as a result of the counselling process. In person-centred practice, a relationship is created in which the client is able to allow experience to manifest itself more clearly in awareness. The client does not need to defend against the sadness, hurt, anger, pain, etc., associated with an experience and so is able to explore the nuances surrounding it that previously may have been prevented from entering into awareness. In allowing themselves to experience these different elements in their fullness, clients are able to evaluate how they feel and think about them and, in turn, clarify their meaning.

Greenberg et al. (1996) state that such cognitive self-examination, which can be termed 'reflexivity', is particular to human consciousness and is an invaluable factor in the change process; yet it is something that is often downplayed by the person-centred approach. Once the client has been able to ascertain what an experience means to them they are then in a position to decide what to do; as Rogers describes in his seven-stage model, clients tend to become more self-responsible as they accurately symbolise more of their experience. In other words, they feel more in control as their process of evaluation shifts from the external to the internal and they make decisions based on their own sound reasoning.

Rogers demonstrates the process

Rogers (1990a) offers one counselling session in particular to demonstrate how and why change occurs within the client. The counselling session took place at a workshop in South Africa and involved one of the participants, Jan. Rogers begins the session by asking Jan what she would like to talk about. Straightaway Rogers is emphasising that he will be taking his lead from the client, a fundamental aspect of the process that he reiterates at several points during the session. Jan states that she has two problems: one, the fear of marriage and having children; and two, the difficulty she experiences in relation to growing older and feeling frightened of what might lie in the future. Rogers asks which of these she would like to start with and she chooses the problem of getting older.

It is interesting to notice the similarity between this and the Gendlin example. In both the client is encouraged to consider what they would like to talk about and are allowed to decide which issue they wish to discuss. For Gendlin, this is achieved through specific stages of focusing, but for Rogers the process occurs more spontaneously, despite the interaction being underpinned by his theoretical approach.

Jan explains how she has begun to feel panic over the last 18 months or so because she is 35 and 40 seems to be coming up fast. Rogers asks if there was anything in particular that happened 18 months ago that might have set this off, and although there was nothing specific, Jan wonders if it might be connected with the fact that her mum died relatively young at the age of 53. She reflects on the fact that her mum died feeling quite bitter about life as she had not done the things she had wanted to do; Jan does not want to end up the same way but is fearful that she might.

At this point in the session Jan asks Rogers to ask her some more questions as she thinks that might help him to get some more information; seeming confused, she says (1990a: 141) 'I just can't – everything is a whirlwind, going round in circles.' But instead of asking her more questions Rogers reflects what she has just said – about things going round so fast in her head that she doesn't know where to begin. He then does ask a question (1990a: 141) but one that is very open-ended: 'I don't know whether you want to talk anymore about your relationship to your mother's life, your fear of that, or what?' This is a crucial point in the process because he is inviting her to go a little deeper into the issue but for *her* to choose what direction that might take: he is inviting her to indwell herself and he is attempting to follow her as closely as he can. This instigates a long pause for reflection on Jan's part and she then begins to focus on the issue of marriage, children and commitment and wonders if these are connected with her sense of unease about growing older. She also identifies that she does not have a fear of commitment generally, with work or friendships for example, but that she experiences it specifically in relation to this issue. Significantly, *Jan* has made this connection and differentiation, not Rogers, and it is an indication that she is beginning to make some sense of her situation. In Rogers' written commentary on the session he makes the following observation at this point to highlight its significance:

> The client 'increasingly differentiates and discriminates the objects of his feelings and perceptions, including … his self, his experience, and the interrelationships between them' (Rogers, 1959: 216). Jan certainly illustrates this statement in my theory as she recognises her fear – not of commitment but only of a special commitment. (Rogers, 1990a: 142)

Jan then goes on to describe how she loves the arts – music and dance in particular – and how she would love to give everything up and devote her life to these things. Because of societal pressures, however, she feels that this is simply not possible. She wonders if this could be linked to her problem. Rogers reflects back to Jan that she seems to have a real sense of purpose about this – that she does want to commit herself to something, i.e. the arts, but feels that she cannot. In his commentary he notes that for someone who seems so uncertain about the future she is obviously clear about her love of the arts, an aspect of herself that now comes to the surface. He states:

> From the point of view of therapeutic process, Jan 'experiences fully, in awareness, feelings which have in the past been denied to awareness, or distorted in awareness' (Rogers, 1959: 216) (Rogers, 1990a: 143)

Jan then goes on to describe how this issue has become more 'vital' for her recently. There is an increased sense of urgency in the way she describes this, as if she is experiencing it at a deeper level. Here she uncovers a new aspect of her experience – a sense of being 'trapped'. Rogers comments:

> It is interesting to follow her search for the right word – the right metaphor – to match her feelings. She has tried out *fear, panic, feelings being vital,* and now *trapped*. Finding a word, phrase, a metaphor that exactly matches the inner felt meaning of the moment helps the client to experience the feeling more fully. (Rogers, 1990a: 144, original italics)

But despite feeling trapped Jan explains how she keeps this to herself and just gets on with life. Then, after a pause in the flow of the conversation, she wonders aloud whether all of this might have something to do with the amateur dramatics she used to be involved with. She reflects that she loves playing the role of the 'naughty little girl' and is aware that if she ever wants something, she usually plays this role in order to obtain it. After a brief interchange with Rogers, she leaves this thought to one side, though, and describes how she wishes that she had someone close that she could go through this whole experience with, someone supportive and encouraging who could help her when it feels too much sometimes. Specifically, she says 'somebody pushing me, saying, you know, "I *know* you can do it, you *can* do it, you *will* do it" … just one person who can believe in me' (1990a: 146, original italics). She laments the fact that she is unable to give this type of positive encouragement to herself, saying that she has tried many times but that it never works. She feels so despondent that she describes it as 'walking into darkness' (1990a: 147) – out of light and into darkness.

At this point Rogers takes a risk and offers what he describes as an intuitive response. Such a response is something that he says he learned to trust over the years – it would often be an observation beyond that which was immediately relevant but nonetheless proved to be therapeutic. Here he says to Jan that he wishes the supportive, encouraging person could be the naughty little girl within Jan that she had mentioned earlier; maybe she could accompany Jan from darkness into light. At first Jan sounds highly sceptical but as Rogers explains himself a little further, Jan discovers that on reflection she feels like she has lost a lot of her naughty little girl – in fact she has disappeared completely! As a result of this realisation she wonders whether despite getting older she can still be that naughty little girl. And leading on from that, she asks if being able to be that naughty little girl might change the way she feels about marriage. They have reached a crucial moment and, just before the session ends, they share this clarification:

Carl: I think that's a very significant question you're asking yourself. If you were a better friend of the little girl inside of you, would that make you less fearful of the risk of marriage? I feel badly that she's been missing for the last eighteen months, I really do.
Jan: (Pause) You're so right. You've really hit the nail on the head. (Rogers, 1990a: 149)

Once again, this is an example of how Rogers does not say what the effect of her actions will be – he firmly believes that *he cannot know* what it will be. Instead he responds by saying that he feels bad that the naughty little girl has been missing for so long, a feeling that she obviously shares too. Judging by her response this matter is of great significance to her: 'You've really hit the nail on the head.'

It is clear there is much similarity between the process of person-centred counselling as demonstrated by Rogers and the process of focusing as illustrated by Gendlin. Indeed, the six steps of focusing – clear a space, felt sense, get a handle, resonate, ask and receive – are, in broad terms, all present within Rogers' session with Jan, although sometimes in a different format. Jan decides what she really wants to talk about, which in turn brings up certain emotional responses for her, which ultimately lead her to identifying the crux of the issue – that she has lost the part of herself that is her 'naughty little girl'. In doing all this she has confronted some of her fears and has found a possible way forward – a way of moving from darkness into light. However, there are some distinct differences between these examples of Rogers' and Gendlin's work. Rogers does not impose a set format on the process, whereas Gendlin and Fay are following a predetermined programme. In focusing, Fay is directed first to concentrate on her bodily felt sense and then to try and analyse what it means; with Jan, the process is not so unidirectional – it involves feelings, thoughts and reflexivity in an interlinking back-and-forth movement. In contrast to Gendlin's more directive role, Rogers tries simply to follow Jan wherever her exploration takes her and plays a far more active part in Jan's experiential world. By empathically and non-judgementally accompanying her, he enables her to move more deeply within herself, gaining a much more accurate symbolisation of her experience. She reaches a deeper understanding of herself through experiencing herself more fully which, although unsettling and frightening at first, ultimately leads her to re-connect with a constructive and restorative aspect of herself that had been missing, much to the detriment of her overall development.

Thus the process of change occurs because Jan is able, within the safety of the relationship, to connect with her experience at a more profound level, differentiating between the elements involved and clarifying what each aspect means to her. This process is possible because the relationship facilitates her movement towards greater self-acceptance. Once this more accurate understanding is achieved she thinks and feels differently about her situation and is clear about what she would like to do in order to change it. Rogers (1990a: 151–2) reports that the next morning Jan spoke to him about the session and said that she had realised there were several parts of herself that had been lost over the previous 18 months. So it would seem that a process of change had been put in motion that would have significant and potentially long-term reverberations.

Rogers (1990a: 151) offers a succinct explanation of why change occurs for Jan when he reflects on how she was able to fully experience her feelings, even though it must have been distressing for her to 'feel the hopelessness of being trapped'. He says: 'Once such a troubling feeling has been felt to its full depth and breadth, one can move on.' This deceptively straightforward process is reminiscent of the Gestalt notion of the 'cycle of gestalt formation and destruction' or 'process of contact', where the constituent elements of each cycle have to be engaged with in order for healthy psychological movement to occur (Mackewn, 1997: 18). Rogers' statement shares this 'complete and move on' quality and could be applied more generally to the counselling process: once a feeling has been fully experienced then movement will occur. This will usually involve some kind of cognitive reflexivity but, bearing in mind Gendlin's perspective, a shift may occur within the body's felt senses, even if this cannot necessarily be described. Perhaps this is simply the way of the actualising tendency: constructive change occurs when an experience is experienced to its fullest extent; the person will change because that is how the tendency actualises.

Summary

With its emphasis on the experiencing of thoughts and feelings more fully, person-centred counselling theory might at first glance seem unlikely to achieve the desired goal of facilitating change within the client. However, building on the philosophical notions of 'being' and 'indwelling', Rogers proposes that the best way to facilitate change is indeed simply to allow clients to explore their experiences at greater depth. It is only through clients indwelling themselves in this way that they can come to understand what their experiences mean to them and therefore how they wish to assimilate and respond to them. An external understanding of their experiences cannot be imposed upon them – indeed it would be counter-productive to attempt to do so; this would simply inhibit rather than facilitate the process.

Thus the focus of the person-centred counsellor is on creating a relationship in which the client can freely explore their experiences. For Gendlin, such a relationship is achieved through the focusing technique but for Rogers, a less structured approach allows the client to explore their thoughts and feelings at their own pace and in their own way. It is only because of the profound sense of acceptance within the relationship, through which the client begins to experience self-acceptance, that this can occur. Crucial throughout this process is the trust placed in the client's ability to determine exactly which experiences need attending to; it is not the counsellor who directs the process in one particular direction or another, it is the client. Through their own reflexivity, the client is able to arrive at a deeper understanding of what their experience means for them and to act accordingly on the basis of that understanding.

Further reading

Gendlin, E.T. (1981) *Focusing* (2nd edition). New York: Bantam Books.
This is a very readable and comprehensive explanation of the focusing technique, offering many examples of how it works and providing much material that is relevant to the person-centred approach as a whole.

Polanyi, M. (1958) *Personal Knowledge: Towards a Post-Critical Philosophy*. London: Routledge & Kegan Paul.
For the interested reader, this work provides a detailed analysis of the author's revolutionary thoughts on the nature of knowledge.
Rogers, C.R. (1990a) 'A Client-Centered/Person-Centered Approach to Therapy' in H. Kirschenbaum and V.L. Henderson (eds), *The Carl Rogers Reader*. London: Constable, pp. 135–52. (Article first published in 1986.)
Rogers offers a full transcript of the interview with Jan and summarises some of the key elements of person-centred counselling that he believes are exemplified by this session.

Some of the factors involved in facilitating change within the client have already been touched upon in previous chapters. But now a more detailed description can be given as to how person-centred theory is actually applied in the counselling setting. The fundamental tenets regarding the practical application of the theory were laid down by Rogers in his two landmark papers of 1957 and 1959. There has been much controversy over the chronological order of these writings and the significance of a slight change in the wording used. But whatever the significance (or not) of these matters, Rogers' hypothesis, in keeping with much of his thinking, is a straightforward yet bold statement that if certain therapeutic conditions exist then psychological change will occur. Interestingly, over the years many different schools of thought have argued that while these conditions are indeed valuable to most therapeutic encounters, they are nothing more than a prelude to the real change-inducing activities that follow. Rogers, however, believes that these conditions are in themselves what engenders change – nothing else needs to be added.

The necessary and sufficient conditions for change

In 1957 Rogers published a paper entitled 'The Necessary and Sufficient Conditions of Therapeutic Change' (Rogers, 1957) in which he states that there are six conditions that are both necessary and sufficient in order to bring about a constructive psychological change within the client. These six conditions are also stated in his 1959 'theory of therapy' (Rogers, 1959), being described here as necessary for therapy to occur. There are slight differences in the wording of these two statements and Wyatt (2001a) helpfully presents an amalgamation of the two, indicating where the differences occur (the 1957 wording appears in brackets):

1 That two persons are in (psychological) contact.
2 That the first person, whom we shall term the client, is in a state of incongruence, being vulnerable, or anxious.
3 That the second person, whom we shall term the therapist, is congruent (or integrated) in the relationship.

4 That the therapist is experiencing unconditional positive regard toward the client.

5 That the therapist is experiencing an empathic understanding of the client's internal frame of reference (and endeavours to communicate this to the client).

6 That the client perceives, at least to a minimal degree, conditions 4 and 5, the unconditional positive regard of the therapist for him, and the empathic understanding of the therapist. (The communication to the client of the therapist's empathic understanding and unconditional positive regard is to a minimal degree achieved.)
   (Wyatt, 2001a: iii)

Confusion has arisen over the chronology of these two papers and also the possible significance of the change in wording – the former potentially influencing the latter. However, there is evidence from Rogers himself, given in a recorded interview (Hart and Tomlinson, 1970), that the 1959 paper was actually written in 1953–4 and thus the 1959 paper precedes the one published in 1957. Furthermore, as Sanders and Wyatt (2001) suggest, the change in wording in the 1957 (later) work does not seem to represent a major shift of clinical importance but is simply a more general formulation of the same hypotheses. Given that the ethos of both works is fundamentally the same, it would seem unlikely that Rogers intended any differences in the wording to be of great significance.

Conditions 1, 2 and 6

Since the publication of these papers the focus of person-centred practitioners has been almost exclusively on conditions 3, 4 and 5 – congruence, unconditional positive regard and empathy – which have come to be known as 'the core conditions'. But what of conditions 1, 2 and 6? Condition 1, 'that two persons are in (psychological) contact' is a condition that seems to have been taken for granted, perhaps as Warner (2001) notes, because Rogers himself treats such contact as an assumption or precondition not needing much explanation. What Rogers (1959: 207) does state is that by 'contact' he means 'the least or minimum experience which could be called a relationship' and so this gives some indication of what he is getting at. However, this description seems woefully inadequate when considering the nature of the relationship that the person-centred approach is trying to engender, i.e. a profound and meaningful relationship. Interestingly, when Rogers had the opportunity to restate his theory some years later (Rogers and Sanford, 1984) 'contact' was not stated as a therapeutic condition. It would seem inaccurate to infer from this that the notion of contact is therefore not important; more likely, Rogers took it to be implicit, given the other conditions, and so considered its mention unnecessary.

With regard to condition 2, this *would* seem to be an obvious prerequisite for any counselling situation because if a person is not in a state of incongruence, why would they feel the need to come for counselling? In terms of the process of change, though, it is of significance that the client is described as 'being vulnerable, or anxious'. Anxiety occurs as a result of the client experiencing threat in relation to material that in some way challenges the current self-concept. As has been discussed earlier, change occurs because the client is able to engage with this material and accurately symbolise it as a result of the therapeutic encounter. Thus, without condition 2 change would be unlikely to occur as a result of person-centred counselling. Rogers' theory relating to incongruence has been explored in previous chapters (see Chapter 3 in particular) so there is no need for further discussion here.

Condition 6 has also been somewhat neglected, maybe because it is viewed as requiring no further explication. Yet it is of profound importance if the relationship is to be capable of producing therapeutic change. The reason for this is straightforward: empathy and unconditional positive regard may be the most awesome therapeutic conditions in the known universe but if the client does not experience them they will be entirely useless! In this sense the intention of the counsellor is unimportant; it is the client's perception of the situation that matters. As Sanders and Wyatt (2001) point out, those theorists who have paid attention to this crucial condition have tended to fall into two camps: those who are content with the general principle of the statement, and those who have attempted to measure the minimum degree to which the client must experience the two conditions in order for them to be effective. Either way, it is the client experience, not that of the counsellor that is of importance. Sanders and Wyatt (2001) provide a culinary metaphor that nicely captures the essence of condition 6:

> …if we wanted to make carrot soup and the recipe read, 'take one carrot', some might understand this to mean 'you can't have carrot soup without a carrot', whilst others would ask 'how big does the carrot have to be before it can really be called carrot soup?' Both would have to agree, though, that if there is no carrot, there is no carrot soup.
>
> The perception of the therapeutic conditions *by the client* is, therefore, key to the whole relationship. Whilst this may be obvious to some, the fact of the matter is that little has been done to explore, document or elaborate understanding of this key element in comparison with empathic understanding, UPR [unconditional positive regard] and congruence. Most of us, it would appear, are content with the reverse logic contained in the assumption, i.e. that since we intend to make carrot soup, then it *must* be a carrot that we are making it with. In other words, since the therapist intends to be empathic and non-judgemental, then this is what the client is perceiving. (Sanders and Wyatt, 2001: 9, original italics)

Given the fundamental importance of condition 6 it seems strange that congruence was not included along with the other two conditions.

However, in a later restatement of his theory (Rogers and Sanford, 1984) Rogers did indeed include congruence in condition 6. Perhaps it was only left out originally because he was concerned that this condition was impossible to measure and so would not have fitted with the research ethos of the time, when the emphasis was firmly on quantitative data and outcome.

Conditions 3, 4 and 5

In terms of therapeutic practice Rogers and the person-centred community generally have placed most emphasis on conditions 3, 4 and 5, often referred to as 'the core conditions'. An enormous amount has been written about these conditions and it is not the intention of this chapter to provide a detailed analysis of each one as this can be found elsewhere (see the Further Reading section at the end of the chapter). However, a brief summary of each condition will now be provided and some of the views and theories pertaining to them will be discussed. While it is not necessary to go into great detail here, a description of how the therapist facilitates the process of change is important in further clarifying how this process occurs.

Rogers likens congruence to 'genuineness' and 'realness', indicating that the counsellor should not be putting up any kind of personal or professional façade (Rogers, 1980). He offers the notion of 'transparency' to capture the essence of this realness – that the counsellor is openly communicating the feelings and attitudes they are experiencing in any given moment. What the counsellor experiences both at gut level and in their awareness, and what is expressed to the client, is all closely matched or is congruent. However, Rogers also states, when describing the counsellor within the counselling relationship, that 'what he or she is experiencing is available to awareness, can be lived in the relationship, and can be communicated, *if appropriate*' (Rogers, 1980: 115, italics added). Thus there would seem to be a discrepancy between the utterly transparent counsellor, who is the open embodiment of everything they are experiencing, and the counsellor who might only openly be themselves if they feel it is appropriate. It would seem that both definitions cannot hold true at the same time – they are mutually exclusive and thus there is inconsistency in Rogers' terminology. As Brodley (1998: 83) notes after reviewing his writings, 'the precise meaning of congruence remains somewhat ambiguous.'

Brodley (1998: 83) warns against the distortions that will occur in person-centred counselling if therapists 'systematically state their own reactions to, or thoughts about, clients' and justify such action by claiming it as congruence. With this in mind, she disagrees with Lietaer (1993) who equates the notion of transparency with counsellor self-disclosure, although it should be stated that Lietaer (1993, 2001a) does not suggest that such communication be made with wanton disregard for the other core conditions. Brodley explains that Rogers (1957) is clear that if the counsellor has a persistent non-therapeutic experience it would be prudent to discuss such experiences with a colleague or supervisor, rather than simply sharing them immediately with the client. Even though Rogers asserted later on (Baldwin, 2000) that should he have such experiences in a counselling situation he would want to express them, Brodley remains convinced that he did not mean a straightforward expression of feelings to the client at the expense of the overall desired therapeutic climate. Quoting Rogers (1959) further, Brodley justifies her stance:

> ...for therapy to occur the wholeness of the therapist in the relationship is primary, but a part of the congruence must be the experience of unconditional positive regard and the experience of empathic understanding. (Rogers, 1959: 215)

For Brodley (1998) there are only four types of situation in which a congruent communication would be made by the counsellor: 1) where the counsellor perceives the client to be confused by inconsistent counsellor behaviour; 2) if the counsellor has persistent experiences that are contrary to the attitudes of empathy or unconditional positive regard, although she urges therapists to exercise great caution in such instances; 3) when the client asks a direct question in relation to the counsellor and it would be disrespectful to the client not to be open; and 4) where a simple and spontaneous disclosure of the counsellor's experience arises as a result of the counsellor's genuine involvement in the relationship.

Whether or not these criteria would be universally considered appropriate, they certainly encompass the major queries involved in the debate on the communication of congruence. More fundamental, perhaps, is the question of whether it should ever be communicated at all because congruence, as Wilkins (1997) notes, is a state of being that can be achieved alone: no relationship is necessary for a state of congruence to exist with oneself. Given the nature of the relationship, though, it is hard to imagine Rogers intended the therapist to be in a congruent state of which the client remains completely unaware. As mentioned above, he did revise the conditions so that congruence was to be perceived by the client along with empathy and unconditional positive regard. And, in any case, he reiterates the notion of being real, genuine and without façade: these are meaningless qualities unless present in the context of the relationship. The debate will no doubt continue as to what should or should not be communicated under the banner of congruence. But it would seem that what Rogers intended was a state of being oneself *in relationship* with the client.

Rogers speaks of unconditional positive regard in terms of 'acceptance, or caring, or prizing' (Rogers, 1980: 116). These terms were an attempt to convey the essential elements of what he meant by an unconditional positive regard: an acceptant and positive attitude on the part of the counsellor to 'whatever the client *is* at that moment' (original italics). Thus the challenge to the counsellor is to experience and communicate a constant level of acceptance to whatever aspect of the client is apparent in any given moment. As Mearns (1994) points out, this is not a question of the counsellor *liking* every client, which would surely be highly unlikely, but of fundamentally accepting them. However, the challenge to the counsellor is still significant and presents several difficulties, one of the most frequently cited being the potential conflict between unconditional positive regard and congruence where the counsellor is experiencing a 'negative' emotion towards the client (Lietaer, 1984; Hendricks, 2001). In addition, there are more general concerns regarding the feasibility of a 'total acceptance' of all aspects of the client; the behaviourists, for example, argue that there will always be selective reinforcement, making such an attitude impossible (Lietaer, 2001b).

Yet the offering of unconditional positive regard is absolutely fundamental to the activity of person-centred counselling and is at the very heart of Rogers' theory. The hypothesis that offering unconditional positive regard to the client results in the client experiencing unconditional positive self-regard is the crux of Rogers' philosophy of therapeutic human interaction and is the mechanism by which the client may begin to symbolise their experience accurately once more. As Rogers states:

> Here is one of the key constructs of the theory, which may be defined in these terms: if the self-experiences of another are perceived by me in such a way that no self-experience can be discriminated as more or less worthy of positive regard than any other, then I am experiencing unconditional positive regard for this individual. To perceive oneself as receiving unconditional positive regard is to perceive that of one's self-experiences none can be discriminated by the other individual as more or less worthy of positive regard. (Rogers, 1959: 208)

This is the foundation stone of his theory of change, as without this attitudinal quality a return to accurate symbolisation is impossible for the client. Accurate symbolisation occurs through a movement towards unconditional positive self-regard and this in turn leads to the client being able to explore their experiences more fully. Indeed, Bozarth (1998: 46) refers to unconditional positive regard as 'the primary change agent' and thus, despite the acknowledged difficulties that offering such an attitude presents, the importance of attempting to achieve this therapeutic condition is indisputable.

The fifth condition concerns empathic understanding, which is often referred to simply as 'empathy'. Rogers describes this condition as being able to sense the feeling and personal meaning of the client's experience – to enter into the client's 'frame of reference'. Empathic understanding is unlikely to remain static, though, and Rogers emphasises the ever-changing nature of empathic understanding as the counsellor continually tests out whether they are accurately perceiving the client on a moment-to-moment basis. When the therapist is functioning well in this sense, it is likely that they will be able to 'clarify not only the meanings of which the client is aware but even those just below the level of awareness' (Rogers, 1980: 116). Thus, if the counsellor can be thought of as accompanying the client on their journey, sometimes the counsellor will be a step ahead, sometimes a step behind and sometimes right there in their shoes with them! The important element within this, of course, is that the counsellor is constantly communicating to the client their sense of what the client is feeling and meaning (as required by condition 6) and adjusting that sense depending on the client's response.

Some researchers and theorists (for example, Truax and Carkhuff, 1967; Mearns and Thorne, 1999) have developed empathy scales in order to measure the accuracy of counsellor empathic responses. Though this is a valuable tool, as it no doubt allows counsellors to hone their skills, particularly in training situations, there is a danger that the highest level on the scale is always seen to be the most desirable. However, while a deeply accurate empathic response – a 'depth reflection' (Mearns and Thorne, 1999: 45) – is undoubtedly highly therapeutic, a sense of when to offer such a response is just as important. As Rogers (1980: 142) states, empathic understanding can involve 'sensing meanings of which he or she [the client] is scarcely aware, but not trying to uncover totally unconscious feelings, since this would be too threatening'.

With this in mind, Bozarth's (1984) notion of 'idiosyncratic modes' of empathy is important as it suggests that effective empathy is not always the classic 'depth reflection' type of response. Bozarth offers his readers a multiple-choice question in order to demonstrate his point:

Which of the following statements is most indicative of an empathic response?

1 I'm having strong sexual feelings toward you.
2 When I took my Volkswagen engine out, the car rolled down the hill, hit the rabbit pen, etc., etc.
3 You feel as though you lost contact with the physical world.
   (Bozarth, 1984: 69–70)

He states that the third answer is the one that would be most commonly thought of as an empathic response but argues that although the other two statements seem highly unlikely candidates, given certain circumstances they may be accurate empathic responses on the part of the counsellor. For example, in relation to the second statement, he describes a counselling situation in which the client has intensely struggled to inform the counsellor of something she 'had to tell' him but remains unable to do so. At their next session, the client begins by asking the counsellor what he has been doing. Intuitively, the counsellor responds by filling up almost the entire session with the problems he had experienced trying to repair his car (even though he gives plenty of opportunities for the client to change the subject if she wishes). Although, at first glance, this does not seem to be an empathic way to respond to the client, she later indicated that she had appreciated his response as he did not try to force her to return to her burning topic, from which she had needed respite. Indeed, 'she identified this action as highly consistent with her "state of being" at the time and later reported that it enabled her to identify the core of her struggle' (Bozarth, 1984: 71).

Thus empathic understanding may be communicated in many different ways but the important element remains the respectful *and* accurate sensing of the client's moment-to-moment experience. The communication of empathic understanding can be highly beneficial to the client, as Rogers observes: 'listening, of this very special kind, is one of the most potent forces for change that I know' (Rogers, 1980: 116). As with unconditional positive regard, though, it presents a substantial challenge to the counsellor:

> To be with another in this way means that for the time being, you lay aside your own views and values in order to enter another's world without prejudice. In some sense it means that you lay aside yourself; this can only be done by persons who are secure enough in themselves that they know they will not get lost in what may turn out to be the strange or bizarre world of the other, and that they can comfortably return to their own world when they wish. (Rogers, 1980: 143)

Each of the core conditions contains within it its own particular qualities and these in turn present different challenges to the counsellor. But perhaps what is most striking, almost 50 years since Rogers first wrote about them, is how interconnected these conditions are both in theory and practice. Each condition on its own possesses acknowledged therapeutic qualities but is vulnerable to misuse and is capable of producing an ultimately counter-therapeutic outcome. Together, they complement one another and enhance their therapeutic value. Rogers intended this relationship from the outset, highlighting, for example, how empathy and unconditional positive regard complement each other:

> Empathic understanding is always necessary if unconditional positive regard is to be fully communicated. If I know little or nothing of you, and experience an unconditional positive regard for you, this means little because further knowledge of you may reveal aspects which I cannot so regard. But if I know you thoroughly, knowing and empathically understanding a wide variety of your feelings and behaviors, and still experience an unconditional positive regard, this is very meaningful. (Rogers, 1959: 231)

Bozarth (2001) confirms the importance of this relationship and no doubt congruence could be added to Rogers' statement above. Indeed, Bozarth (1998: 43) takes the relational quality of the core conditions a stage further, arguing that 'Genuineness and empathic understanding are viewed as two contextual attitudes for the primary condition of change; i.e., unconditional positive regard.' This notion that unconditional positive regard is the primary quality that instigates change is echoed by other writers (for example, Bozarth and Wilkins, 2001a; Freire, 2001). Whether or not this is true, and it would seem to make sense given the wider context of Rogers' theory and the causes of psychological maladjustment, what remains clear is that the necessary and sufficient conditions will best bring about change when they are combined together as a unified whole.

Summary

Rogers' six 'necessary and sufficient conditions' define what he believes to be required in order for therapeutic change to occur. Most attention, by Rogers and other person-centred writers, has been focused on conditions 3, 4 and 5 – congruence, unconditional positive regard and empathic understanding – often referred to as 'the core conditions'. But recently there has been increasing emphasis on the fact that there are six conditions, not three, and that conditions 1, 2 and 6 cannot simply be ignored. This is, perhaps, particularly true of condition 6 as without the effective communication of unconditional positive regard and empathy (and congruence, which was later added), the attitudinal qualities of the therapist will have little or no impact and change is unlikely to occur.

The demands that are placed on the counsellor in attempting to offer these conditions to the client are considerable. But where the counsellor is successful and is able to create the desired therapeutic environment, utilising all of the conditions discussed, change will occur as the client is able to explore their experiences more fully. As a result of the relationship the client discovers an increased openness to their experiences and although this initially may involve much painful exploration, it will ultimately lead to a new and more satisfying way of being.

Further reading

Wyatt, G. (ed.) (2001b) *Rogers' Therapeutic Conditions: Evolution, Theory and Practice. Volume 1: Congruence.* Ross-on-Wye: PCCS Books.
Haugh, S. and Merry, T. (eds) (2001) *Rogers' Therapeutic Conditions: Evolution, Theory and Practice. Volume 2: Empathy.* Ross-on-Wye: PCCS Books.
Bozarth, J.D. and Wilkins, P. (eds) (2001) *Rogers' Therapeutic Conditions: Evolution, Theory and Practice. Volume 3: Unconditional Positive Regard.* Ross-on-Wye: PCCS Books.
Wyatt, G. and Sanders, P. (eds) (2001) *Rogers' Therapeutic Conditions: Evolution, Theory and Practice. Volume 4: Contact and Perception.* Ross-on-Wye: PCCS Books.
This series of books, published by PCCS, contains a wealth of information with contributions from a variety of writers. The books contain a wide array of different presentations on theory and practice and provide a thought-provoking resource for anyone wishing to delve deeper into each subject.

Mearns, D. and Thorne, B. (1999) *Person-Centred Counselling in Action* (2nd edition). London: Sage.
This book provides an excellent outline of the main elements involved in the theory and practice of person-centred counselling with separate chapters focusing on congruence, unconditional positive regard and empathy.

The previous chapter outlined 'the necessary and sufficient conditions for therapeutic change' as described by Rogers primarily in his 1957 and 1959 papers. Initially research evidence suggested that his hypothesis was correct – that these conditions were indeed necessary and sufficient. But, as Bozarth (1998) reports, by the end of the 1960s it was increasingly asserted that while the conditions were necessary, and the focus was very much on congruence, unconditional positive regard and empathic understanding, they were not sufficient in themselves. There has been an ongoing debate since then (still running) over whether the conditions are necessary *and* sufficient, with argument and counter-argument being presented with equal determination (for example, Orlinsky and Howard, 1987; Patterson, 1984). Wilkins (2003) summarises some of the main arguments within the debate while Bozarth (1998) arrives at the following overview:

> There is virtually no direct research that supports the position that the attitudinal qualities are necessary but not sufficient and something else is needed for therapeutic personality change. … The conclusion of necessary but not sufficient as it emerges from the research is, at best, a quantum leap of interpretation. (Bozarth, 1998: 38)

Bozarth identifies the fundamental problem underpinning the criticism of Rogers' hypothesis as the inability of therapists and researchers (from orientations other than the person-centred approach) to embrace the notion that the counsellor does not *have* to intervene in the client's process in order to set them moving in the right direction. The belief in the client's self-determination is untenable for such critics and therefore the conditions, by definition, cannot be sufficient. However, Bozarth (1998: 41) does propose that the conditions may not be *necessary* since he is aware that individuals have undergone change as a result of 'experiencing a religious conversion, a sunset, a smile, a traumatic experience, and so on', a view explored and developed by Purton (2002). For Bozarth, such a view is plausible because of the nature of the actualising tendency and the growth and movement that occurs within all living beings despite any adverse conditions that may be present.

This is an important fact to embrace, even if it is an uncomfortable one for therapists to engage with: change occurs without counselling! In the latter stages of his life, though, Rogers did not focus on what might be possible *without* the therapeutic encounter but instead further immersed himself in his exploration of what might enhance the process of change within the counselling relationship. In his later writing (1980), reflecting on his practice, he describes a new element in his counselling work that he believes has a profoundly therapeutic effect. This is something that is difficult to pinpoint and for which there can be little quantitative research. But this does not deter him from believing it to be important:

> When I am at my best, as a group facilitator or as a therapist, I discover another characteristic. I find that when I am closest to my inner, intuitive self, when I am somehow in touch with the unknown in me, when perhaps I am in a slightly altered state of consciousness, then whatever I do seems to be full of healing. Then simply my *presence* is releasing and helpful to the other. There is nothing I can do to force this experience, but when I can relax and be close to the transcendental core of me, then I may behave in strange and impulsive ways in the relationship, ways which I cannot justify rationally, which have nothing to do with my thought processes. But these strange behaviors turn out to be *right*, in some odd way: it seems that my inner spirit has reached out and touched the inner spirit of the other. Our relationship transcends itself and becomes a part of something larger. Profound growth and healing and energy are present.
> (Rogers, 1980: 129, original italics)

Rogers considers that this 'presence' is a phenomenon that he and others have perhaps underestimated, describing it as having a mystical and spiritual quality (Rogers, 1980). The example of Rogers' work with a client, Jan, in Chapter 5 demonstrates what he means when he uses phrases such as 'intuitive self'. Rogers seems to be saying that such a state of mind occurs where he is able to let go of his usual process of cognition, where perhaps he would be thinking logically and rationally, and align himself more closely with his own bodily intuition. Bowen (1986) has also written of this type of therapeutic interaction and how it can be enormously facilitative (McMillan, 1997). She describes working with a client for about three months, during which time the client had relayed her painful story with very little emotion. A central issue for the client was that she felt her mother should have protected her from her abusive stepfather, with whom she continued to have a difficult relationship. Then in one session, while the client was describing an upsetting episode with her stepfather, the counsellor saw an image of a monkey over the client's shoulder. Such an image occurred completely out of the blue – monkeys had never been mentioned by the client and they held no significance for the counsellor. After deliberating over whether to mention this she decided to say something and asked the client if monkeys held any particular meaning for her. After a slight pause the startled client burst into tears, exclaiming that her mother used to call her 'little monkey' and that her mother was also terrified by her stepfather. Clearly the counsellor could not have known of the significance of monkeys to the client and yet by some form of connection between the two, the counsellor's intuition proved to be correct. Thus something beyond words and logic had occurred; what happened could not be defined scientifically nor could it have been foreseen.

The elusive quality of presence

What Rogers is describing in the above extract, however, goes beyond the use of intuition, and that is not to underestimate the importance of intuitive responses. He is describing a profound meeting of two people whereby a transcendental connection is made between the deepest parts of their beings, so profound in fact that their relationship 'becomes a part of something larger' and enters into some kind of spiritual mutuality. Moore (2001) reflects that Rogers' description of such a profound experience had troubled her for years as a therapist because it seemed an incomprehensible and impossible ideal. But then, unexpectedly, she experienced the type of experience he mentions when she was working with a long-standing client. This was a client (Lucy) whom she saw over three and a half years for a total of 47 sessions; the session that proved so significant was session 46. Moore and her client agreed to make a joint presentation to a group of counsellors-in-training describing their work together, and so the client's experience of session 46 is available in written form. Moore (2001) quotes from both the client's and her own account as she considers what occurred between them:

[Lucy:] The distance in time between what we were talking about and the present seemed to suddenly collapse, and we were looking at and feeling my present emotions and perceptions. Judy [Moore] mentioned that I was still seeing 'being all right' as a fixed state that I was yet to arrive at, and sparks began to fly in my mind as connections were made. All my counselling with Judy, the experience of the Associates' Programme [a person-centred self-development course], some of my academic work on changing perceptions of the self, so much of my experience, seemed to suddenly be pulled together and then flip into a whole, a calm fundamental change in perception. My perception of myself and others radically shifted. Rather than seeing those that had arrived and those that hadn't, I felt all as moving, changing. I suddenly felt that I could be OK now, with all my anxieties, fears and embarrassments, rather than looking to a future point where they just didn't happen to me! ... When I walked out of the counselling centre I felt a qualitative change in everything. ... We were both aware that what had happened was so significant and fundamental. I really feel it is amazing and wonderful that we were able to share perceptions so closely in the session that it could lead me into such an enormous shift.

[Moore:] Lucy said that she felt she 'should' be OK now, having done the Associates' Programme. It occurred to me at this point that she was seeing growth in terms of 'arrival' at a fixed point rather than as a constantly-changing process and I said this. I remember Lucy dissolving as if she was completely overwhelmed by the revelation. I can remember but can't begin to do justice to the strength of the emotion that took over the session. ...It seemed as if she was allowing herself to be the process that she had hitherto understood to be a desirable state and I became swept up in that process. (Moore, 2001: 200–1)

Reflecting on these extracts, Moore (2001: 201) comments that she 'can still remember, even at a distance of six years, that I 'dissolved' as Lucy 'dissolved' and that we were *both* being whatever it was that was happening' (original italics). It seems both she and the client experienced an incredible sense of mutuality, that somehow they had tapped into something that was much larger than the simple meeting of two people. The client's experience transcended anything that she had experienced previously as she perceived 'a qualitative change in everything'. Thus many of the qualities Rogers describes were present in the moment for Moore and her client. Interestingly, a fundamental point of Rogers' theory of change also seemed to play an important part in the client's shift – the notion that change is not concerned with fixed points in the future but with ongoing process. However, despite this element of his theory leading us in the direction of understanding how such moments in counselling occur, Rogers does not actually describe in any detail how or why such moments of transcendence come about, which is perhaps why Moore had struggled to experience or comprehend this notion of presence.

Bozarth (1998: 83) takes the view that the actualising tendency is 'the fundamental curative factor lying within the person' and this tendency can presumably be considered as accounting for any such phenomenon occurring. Geller and Greenberg (2002) interviewed some 'expert therapists' about their understanding of presence and concluded that presence is 'viewed as a foundation and necessary precondition to the relationship conditions of empathy, congruence and unconditional positive regard' (2002: 85). Indeed they suggest that presence is the embodiment of these relationship conditions, something that Rogers seems to hint at when he states:

> Perhaps it is something around the edges of those conditions that is really the most important element of therapy – when my self is very clearly, obviously present. (Baldwin, 2000: 30)

Drawing on the participants' responses, Geller and Greenberg (2002: 75–82) identify three main stages in their model of therapeutic presence: preparing the ground for presence, process of presence and experiencing presence. In this latter stage they group the responses into four main aspects: *immersion*, involving the counsellor being 'intimately engaged and absorbed in the experience of the moment'; *expansion*, characterised by 'a sense of inner spaciousness and even joy, accompanied by the experience of flow, energy and calm'; *grounding*, relating to a sense of being 'centered in one's self and one's own personal existence'; and *being with and for the client*, which involves a profound compassion and respect for the client. They conclude that presence 'involves a *being* with the client rather than a *doing* to the client' (original italics).

Clearly Moore (2001) has found what Geller and Greenberg term 'immersion' to be of most interest, turning to the work of Gendlin (1981, 1996) and André Rochais, who founded the PRH Organisation (Pérsonnalité et Rélations Humaines). Both these lines of theory and practice have less of an emphasis on the notion of the self, which Moore believes to be a limiting theoretical construct, and focus more on the experiencing of the moment and attempting to achieve a profound and unconditional acceptance of whatever is there in that moment. Rochais, in particular, believes this will lead to experiencing of a transcendental nature, as Moore (2001: 207) observes: 'That simple acceptance of what is there, according to the PRH system, eventually opens the person to the pure unconditional positive regard of transcendent reality.'

Presence through tenderness

While Moore has found that the practice of Soto Zen Buddhism deepens her understanding of this quality still further, Thorne, coming from a different spiritual perspective, namely Christianity, finds such moments of transcendence as described by Rogers to be the result of a profound trust. This trust occurs because of a particular quality that the counsellor endeavours to provide, the quality of tenderness (Thorne, 1991). The word 'tender' best captures the elements of the experience Thorne is trying to describe, as for him 'it seems effortlessly to bridge the worlds of the material and carnal, of the feelings and emotions, of the moral and spiritual, of suffering and of healing, of youth and age, of active and passive. It is, if you like, a supremely holistic word' (Thorne, 1991: 75). Some similarity between the broad area of interest of Rogers and Thorne is therefore already apparent but this goes further when Thorne describes the quality of tenderness as demonstrating a 'preparedness and an ability to move between the worlds of the physical, the emotional, the cognitive and the mystical without strain' (Thorne, 1991: 76). Thus the mystical and transcendental qualities are also common to both. Furthermore, the notion of mutuality is present, with Thorne describing the experience as follows:

> At such a moment I have no hesitation in saying that my client and I are caught up in a stream of love. Within this stream there comes an effortless or intuitive understanding and what is astonishing is how complex this understanding can be. It sometimes seems that I receive my client whole and thereafter possess a knowledge of him or her which does not depend on biographical data. This

understanding is intensely personal and invariably it affects the self-perception of the client and can lead to marked changes in attitude and behaviour. For me as a counsellor, it is accompanied by a sense of joy which, when I have checked it out, has always been shared by the client. (Thorne, 1991: 77)

And a little later he adds:

It appears increasingly to me that, when I can be tender or when I experience tenderness in another, neither I nor they can any longer be satisfied with a fragmented existence. We no longer wish to be mere facets of ourselves, and as a result we find the courage to cross the bridge into new areas which had previously been hidden or feared. What is more, the other person is perceived not as a threat to our own wholeness, but as a beloved companion who is on the same journey. We are truly members one of another. (Thorne, 1991: 78)

So counsellor and client can be 'members one of another' and joyful in that mutuality. Such union and transformation is possible because of what he sees as the 'liberating paradox'. So often a paradox becomes a trap where the seemingly 'either–or' option holds no genuine gain. But where such paradox can be converted to 'both–and' the outcome can be profoundly different. Tenderness can provide the means by which such paradox is liberated, for it is in itself the harmonious expression of supposed contradictions – that of weakness and strength, fragility and constancy. It is in such moments that profound change can occur. Thorne's understanding of the process has been greatly aided by the work of the monk, Dom Sebastian Moore (Moore, 1982). Thorne summarises Moore's interpretation of the Genesis story of the Fall as concerning first a distrust in God, which then leads to shame and a distrust in one's body. For Thorne, this sets up an endless cycle of distrusting God, then our bodies, then our desires that we vainly seek to control, which leads to guilt and an attempt at reconciliation with God, which ultimately leads once again to distrust in God, and so on. The only way to break free of the cycle is through the liberating paradox of tenderness which, in the moment of being experienced, allows trust in God, trust in our bodies and our desires, and so allows us to be completely free of shame. Therefore 'we are restored to full friendship with God or, in secular terms, we know that we are born to be lovers and to be loved' (Thorne, 1991: 80). Thus in spiritual and secular terms the person is liberated by a profound sense of being accepted. It is in such moments of profound acceptance that transformation can occur.

Presence: a profound acceptance?

In their search for a deeper understanding of Rogers' notion of presence and his description of moments where the 'relationship transcends itself and becomes a part of something larger', both Moore (2001) and Thorne

(1991) have explored writings beyond the work of Rogers and the person-centred approach. Spiritual texts and beliefs have enabled them to comprehend the process at a deeper level. For Moore, this concerns 'an acceptance of the truth of the present moment', something that is facilitated by the practice of a particular strand of Buddhism; for Thorne, it concerns liberation through tenderness, which allows the client a profound feeling of being reunited with God and leaving the individual, for a moment at least, completely free of shame. In essence, these descriptions are both extensions of Rogers' notion of acceptance but go beyond the little explanation he provides as to why or how such profound and healing experiences occur. They offer alternative explanations as to the nature of such experiences and enhance the discussion regarding this extraordinary phenomenon. However, as Geller and Greenberg (2002) suggest, presence might best be thought of as the embodiment of the relationship conditions of empathy, unconditional positive regard and congruence when combined to produce their most profound effect, something that Rogers himself at least hints at (Baldwin, 2000). Thorne (2002) clearly believes that this is indeed what Rogers is suggesting and yet, at the same time, he acknowledges that:

> Profound spiritual experiences cannot be planned and predicted, and it would be foolish in the extreme to imagine that person-centred therapists can somehow be equipped to meet their clients in such a way that a transformational and transcendent experience is guaranteed. (Thorne, 2002: 37)

Therefore it is not the case that the establishment of certain therapeutic conditions will automatically result in a transcendent experience – but their existence would seem to greatly enhance the possibility of such an experience occurring. No doubt there is much discussion still to be had concerning the nature and quality of presence.

Summary

Since Rogers first published his hypotheses regarding the 'necessary and sufficient conditions' there has been much debate as to whether they are indeed necessary and/or sufficient, a debate that continues to this day. Bozarth (1998) offers a considered response, concluding that they may not be necessary but are always sufficient. Rogers (1980), however, became less concerned with proving his hypotheses to be right in the latter stages of his life and work and instead reflected on what he believed to be the underestimated role that transcendental qualities have to play in the therapeutic encounter. In certain moments during such encounters he believes that a qualitative shift occurs which enables the relationship to 'transcend itself' and 'become a part of something larger'. In these moments he has experienced 'profound growth and healing'.

Although Rogers did not go into detail about how such moments come about, writers like Moore (2001) and Thorne (1991, 2002) have incorporated spiritual perspectives into their understanding of why these moments occur. Perhaps, though, Rogers did not attempt to describe this phenomenon because it is by its nature indescribable. For much of his professional life Rogers found himself having to construct hypotheses in a format that could be subjected to the accepted standards of scientific psychology. Within this realm of the transcendental, though, Rogers found a way of being that was highly facilitative, even though it was not something he could fully describe, let alone explain. In allowing himself this freedom from explanation, he has left an important legacy for the person-centred community to further explore. Whether or not presence is the relationship conditions of empathy, unconditional positive regard and congruence working together in their most potent form remains a matter of some debate. What is likely, is that this elusive and yet highly facilitative quality will continue to fascinate for many years to come.

Further reading

Rogers, C.R. (1980) *A Way of Being*. Boston: Houghton Mifflin.
This later work of Rogers contains his thoughts on the quality of presence. Written in a less formal and scientific style than earlier works, it is a very readable presentation of his ideas and experiences.

Moore, J. (2001) 'Acceptance of the Truth of the Present Moment as a Trustworthy Foundation for Unconditional Positive Regard' in J.D. Bozarth and P. Wilkins (eds), *Rogers' Therapeutic Conditions: Evolution, Theory and Practice. Volume 3: Unconditional Positive Regard*. Ross-on-Wye: PCCS Books, pp. 198–209.
Thorne, B. (1991) *Person-Centred Counselling: Therapeutic and Spiritual Dimensions*. London: Whurr.
Thorne, B. (2002) *The Mystical Power of Person-Centred Therapy: Hope Beyond Despair*. London: Whurr.
These three works offer thoughtful and insightful discussion on the qualitative nature of the counsellor's presence and the effect this may have on the therapeutic relationship.

The counsellor and the counselling relationship may not be necessary for change, given the discussion in the previous chapter, but such a relationship can be enormously facilitative if it enables the client to develop a greater sense of self-acceptance. Rogers' radical notion of change – that change is an ongoing process rather than a transformation from one fixed state to another – is only possible if clients are able to experience themselves more fully, allowing into awareness all aspects of their experience. But in today's society clients face a vast array of external conditions and influences that make accepting themselves and their experiences an extraordinarily difficult task.

Positive regard in today's society

Every person needs to receive positive regard and yet we rarely receive it unconditionally simply for being ourselves. Consequently we all adapt our thoughts, feelings and behaviours in order to receive positive regard from others, leaving our own inner valuing process to one side and taking on external values that become our conditions of worth. These external values come from many different sources, not just parents or 'significant others'. As long ago as the 1960s, Rogers was aware of the variety of influences that were in operation within society and how confusing these were for individuals trying to experience themselves more fully and reconnect with the actualising tendency within them. In addition to identifying parents, family, teachers, religion and politics as being sources of conditions of worth he mentions the role of the media as an important force in this relationship. Coca-Cola, chewing gum, refrigerators and cars were the desirable products of the day, which Rogers sums up as the 'Coca-Cola culture' (Rogers, 1973: 18). If it was influential in the 1960s, it is easy to appreciate the significance of the media today with our 24/7 lifestyle. Twenty-four-hour channels and programme schedules mean that television never sleeps and we are constantly subjected to a variety of images and messages about how we should live our lives.

People, and young people in particular, are bombarded by this implicit and explicit conditioning, which attempts to convince them they should be whatever the particular product or, perhaps more accurately, particular brand name says they should be. As Klein (2001: 4) identifies, corporations now claim that producing goods is only an incidental part of their operation: what companies produce primarily are not things 'but *images of their brands*' (original italics). 'Branding', the adopted buzzword to describe this process, took on a new perspective with the advent of the all-music television channel, MTV. In addition to promoting music and advertising products, it sold itself – it sold MTV. As Klein (2001: 44) explains: 'though there have been dozens of imitators since, the original genius of MTV, as every marketer will tell you, is that viewers didn't watch individual shows, they simply watched MTV.'

There is little doubt that the MTV generation is subjected to the most sophisticated and exhaustive presentation of 'image', more so than any generation before it. If we transpose Rogers' comments about the 1960s to the beginning of the twenty-first century, some of the desirable products of today are: clothes (including sportswear), computers and other 'hi-tech' gadgets, cars (still highly desirable 40 years on), mobile phones and TV game consoles (including the games to go with them). All of this might be summed up as 'the satellite/cable TV culture'. Some of the persuasive messages of this culture can be identified as follows:

> It is of primary importance to be 'cool'. This is implied in so many different ways through TV programmes and advertisements, but might include looking a certain way (in appearance), having the 'right' label clothes, having the 'right' mobile phone (as with any hi-tech product, this usually means the latest version of it), etc.

> It is important to be sexually desirable – particularly for women. A number of messages are contained within this condition including: it is important to be slim, to be physically fit and toned, to have well-groomed hair, etc. Again, these are particularly, although not exclusively, important for women.

> It is important to be able to perform tasks quickly – and to be seen to do so effortlessly. 'Instant messaging', a feature heavily promoted in the sale of mobile phones, would seem to sum up this command. Being able to communicate quickly and immediately is a defining factor of this generation.

> Following on from this, it is important for you to be able to communicate instantly wherever you are – so communication devices must be mobile, hence mobile phones and laptop computers.

> Style is more important than substance. The image of how you 'look' drinking coffee in a café or your home is more important than how the coffee actually tastes. The image of how you 'look' using your mobile phone or laptop computer is more important than its functionality (although its immediacy is a prerequisite).

All of these factors (and the list could go on) become persuasive conditions of worth on the individual, relentlessly imploring them to look, behave and 'be' a certain way. The emphasis now placed on branding and image in the media means that a person's entire lifestyle is being conditionally regarded, rather than one particular choice or aspect of behaviour. This is a significant change in the way the media relates to us and intensifies its ability to influence us. Companies and organisations increasingly attempt to sell their version of how a person should behave in all aspects of their lives, not simply influence choice in relation to an isolated product. The 'way of being' for sale, though, is very different from that which Rogers is advocating for a fulfilling way of life. Rogers' basic striving, for a person to be able to accept themselves for whoever they are, is a far cry from the implicit and explicit requests via television to conform to a certain way of being in order to be acceptable. Positive self-regard will remain elusive for those who do not, and perhaps cannot, fit the external conditions of worth presented in this way.

From modernism to postmodernism

Another way in which the media impacts on the individual of today is to cause confusion. However, such confusion is not simply a result of the media, although this clearly has a role to play, as shall be discussed in a moment. The confusion is as much about the pace and style of life at the beginning of the twenty-first century. But in order to try and understand how society reached this current state, first it is necessary to consider what preceded it. Modernism, broadly speaking, is the term used to define the period of history in western culture from the end of the eighteenth century to the middle of the twentieth century. It is a period characterised by enormous advances in science and industrial production that led to an era of certainty – an age of belief in humankind's ability to ascertain absolute truths about knowledge and the physical world. As Gergen describes (1992: 18), 'As it appeared, human beings were on the verge of mastering the fundamental order of the universe.' In stark contrast, postmodernism, the term used to define our current era, is defined by uncertainty and rejects any notion of absolute truths that are simply waiting to be discovered. Instead it suggests that truth is not absolute but is open to construction and interpretation.

It is difficult to state exactly when the change from modernism to postmodernism occurred, but Kvale (1992a) offers the end of the Second World War as a conclusive moment in the transition of how we think and act in the world. After the atrocities of that war, all the sense of progress and achievement through human knowledge and application became meaningless. It was all a lie. He explains:

Modernity places man in the centre, and sees man as a rational being. There is a basic assumption of emancipation and progress through reason and science. The faith in emancipation through more knowledge dissolved in 1945, if not before then. After Auschwitz and Hiroshima it has become difficult to uphold a belief in general progress of mankind through more rationality and science. (Kvale, 1992a: 32)

Postmodernism is characterised, then, by a sense of uncertainty about the future and a rejection of the idea of progress through scientific knowledge (Sarup, 1996). We are no longer on the road to universal truth under the steam of our own indubitable, ever-increasing knowledge; in our post-modern times there is no yellow brick road, no single path to an idyllic future. In the pluralistic society of today there are differing views about how truth is considered and defined, each competing with the other; now there are several truths to choose from, not one that is universally accepted.

The yearning for certainty, however, can still be seen within society. The focus of cosmologists towards the end of the last century, for example, was to discover a unifying theory that would allow all humankind to know the 'truth' of the universe – and there is no sign of this drive diminishing as we begin the new millennium. This yearning for truth is epito-mised by the work of the cosmologist Stephen Hawking, now a household name, and is summarised by the much-quoted final paragraph of his best-selling *A Brief History of Time*:

However, if we do discover a complete theory, it should in time be understand-able in broad principle by everyone, not just a few scientists. Then we shall all, philosophers, scientists, and just ordinary people, be able to take part in the question of why it is that we and the universe exist. If we find the answer to that, it would be the ultimate triumph of human reason – for then we would know the mind of God. (Hawking, 1988: 175)

Other fields of scientific interest, though, such as quantum theory, where the emphasis is on parallel existences, even multiple parallel existences and therefore uncertainty as to outcome, demonstrate how the assured optimism of modernism is no longer the dominant ideology it once was. Within our society there may still be a yearning for certainty through knowledge but such desire is no longer accompanied by an unassailable faith in the outcome.

Uncertainty and confusion in a postmodern world

A world without truth and certainty is a confusing one, full of conflicting ideas and images that can leave a person bereft of a sense of meaning or understanding. Gergen (1991) describes this type of existence as *multi-phrenia* and believes it to be a major psychological problem of our time.

Baudrillard uses the term *hyperreality* to describe a world of 'simulations' where 'simulation … is the generation by models of a real without origin or reality: a hyperreal' (Baudrillard, 1996: 76). What Baudrillard is suggesting is that in this era of postmodernism society operates on the notion of *sign values*. Products no longer have any real worth or function but instead provide prestige amongst peers and acquire certain meanings among particular social groups. The 'Air Jordan' training shoe, produced by the sports manufacturer Nike, provides a good example of a sign value in operation: expensive, 'street-cred' and not really worn for the purpose for which they were supposedly designed. The advertising slogan prompted the consumer's desire to own the status symbol of 'Nike Air Jordan': it read 'get some get some get some get some' (Appignanesi and Garratt, 1999). The consumer was manipulated into thinking they could be like the basketball player, Michael Jordan, who, through a series of sophisticated advertisements appeared to be able to fly as he scored a basket. The shoes were not bought simply in order to play basketball, though – the consumer wanted to be imbued with an association with Michael Jordan and the Nike brand, as well as ensuring acceptance among peers and fellow consumers.

Rappoport et al. (1999: 95) summarise Baudrillard's view as a general rule that states: 'the intrinsic properties of objects and events have become less significant than their sign qualities (the designer label on clothing can be more important than its fit or comfort).' Thus individuals are caught up in a world where sign values denote what is important. In such a world of simulations it is increasingly difficult to distinguish what is real and not real, good and bad, true and false. It is not surprising that the notion of some kind of truth, some kind of certainty, is still very desirable for some, as demonstrated by its pursuit in certain scientific fields of inquiry. On a day-to-day basis, even the most self-assured individual can be left bewildered. Klein (2001) cites some research by Fox (1995) that demonstrates the effect of this confusion. Fox found that the majority of 200 Missouri high-school pupils who watched American TV's Channel One as part of their class activity thought that sports stars paid shoe companies to be in their commercials! Fox concluded from this that the children were unable to evaluate accurately the relationships within advertising on television. However, Klein (2001) wonders whether these and other children can actually comprehend the true relationship of sponsorship and branding more accurately than adults can. Michael Jordan became a brand in his own right with huge influence over the sales of Nike's and other companies' products; it was not simply a case of Michael Jordan being a vehicle for Nike to promote its products – Nike and other companies became a vehicle for Michael Jordan. The notion of who owns who, or who is manipulating who, is no longer clear cut.

For Sarup (1996) the effect of all this is to produce a sort of collapsing and dissolving of our sense of boundaries of time and space. So much of the world is presented to us through television that it becomes impossible to distinguish what is real and what is image: the two merge. Sarup's concern is that since identity is related to what we are not, 'the other', then how can we conceive of our identity if there is no difference by which to judge it? This echoes others' views on identity, such as Gregg (1995: 637), who states: 'identity must not be viewed as a set of self-attributions. ... Instead, identity consists of a system of self versus anti-self, or Me versus not-Me contrasts, so the meaning of a quality attributed to Me cannot be known without discovering the contrary not-Me representations(s) which define it' (quoted in Cooper, 1999: 62). When the media blurs and confuses experience to such an extent that it is hard to know what is real and not real, how can the Me and the not-Me be clear?

Engaging with the complexities of postmodern life

In order to engage successfully with such a world, Rappoport et al. (1999) argue that the individual requires a pluralistic sense of self, one that is capable of responding to and negotiating the milieu that is postmodern life. They draw a distinction between serial and simultaneous pluralism. The former refers to the generally accepted premise that as individuals move through the different stages of their life-span they accordingly adapt their concept of self in relation to their experience, such as careers, relationships, geographic locations and environments, etc. Simultaneous pluralism, however, suggests that the individual in postmodern times has available a 'dynamic portfolio' of self-concepts that are available *within* each stage of their life. This is similar to Mearns' (1999, 2002; Mearns and Thorne, 2000) notion of 'configurations of self', as discussed in previous chapters, although Mearns is not saying such configurations exist purely as a result of postmodernism. The problem, of course, is how the individual maintains a healthy balance between these different conceptualisations or configurations of self and avoids being overwhelmed by postmodern complexity and the potential lack of psychological cohesion that follows. O'Hara and Anderson (1996) offer an example from their client work, showing how difficult it is to keep that balance and not feel overwhelmed:

> Then there's Beverley, who comes into therapy torn between two lifestyles and two identities. In the California city where she goes to college, she is a radical feminist; on visits to her Midwestern home town she is a nice, sweet, square, conservative girl. The therapist asks her when she feels most like herself. She says, 'when I'm on the airplane.' (O'Hara and Anderson, 1996: 167)

Beverley is just one example cited by O'Hara and Anderson but they feel her experience is shared by many, viewing her and others as:

> ... shoppers in the great marketplace of realities that the contemporary western world has become: here a religion, there an ideology, over there a lifestyle. They,

and millions like them, browse among a vast array of possibilities and in the process change not only their beliefs but their beliefs about belief – their ideas about what truth is and where it is found. They change not only their identities (I'm a woman, I'm a Jew, I'm a Jungian, I'm a liberal, I'm a Libra) but their ideas about what identity means. Some enjoy the freedom that can be found in this, some try to escape from the freedom and some are nearly destroyed by it. (O'Hara and Anderson, 1996: 167)

Thus O'Hara and Anderson see the complexity of postmodern life affecting individuals at the most profound level, leading them to question not only their own identity but also what the notion of identity itself actually means. For some this freedom to question such profound issues will be a liberating chance for exploration but for many it will prove overwhelming, causing them to seek methods of escape in order to avoid psychological annihilation.

The challenges facing the client

These are the challenges, then, that face the client at the beginning of the twenty-first century. Most of the needs and difficulties described by Rappoport et al. (1999) and O'Hara and Anderson (1996) are acknowledged in Rogers' writings and reflect the fundamental problems facing any person as described by Rogers. As mentioned at the beginning of this chapter, Rogers acknowledged the difficulties facing people a generation or more ago in the 1960s and his fundamental beliefs about what hinders a person's development are perhaps even more relevant today. Rappoport et al. (1999) describe the need for 'simultaneous pluralism'; at the heart of Rogers' theory is the notion of continual changingness, a fluidity that permeates the individual who would have the necessary adeptness for postmodern living. By definition, Rogers' notion is one that fits any context, for the individual's openness to experience allows adaptation to any and all experience. This is by no means easy, though, as Rogers (1973: 23) recognises: 'The process is complex, the choices often very perplexing and difficult, and there is no guarantee that the choice which is made will in fact prove to be self-actualising.' And the greater the complexity of situations and experiences, of course, the more this is relevant. Indeed, the myriad of influences on identity and the resulting effect as described by O'Hara and Anderson (1996) would, again, be in keeping with Rogers' viewpoint. For Rogers, the disconnection with the person's own valuing process engenders insecurity and anxiety. The source of positive regard remains external and unreliable, instigating uncertainty about what the changing environment will bring. This in turn leads to a more rigid and inflexible sense of self because the individual is unable to adapt freely due to a lack of positive self-regard and the reliance on external factors for self-validation.

In a way, it seems that Rogers anticipated that postmodern living would simply exacerbate the already existing difficulties confronting a person. Rappoport et al. (1999: 94) describe postmodernity, at least at the level of popular culture, as 'a condition of flux, multiplicity, and transformation: whatever "is" today, is not likely to be the same tomorrow'. There is no doubt that such a rate of change combined with a multiplicitous experience can lead to confusion, anxiety and a desperate attempt to grasp and hold on to whatever external affirmation can be identified. It is ironic that at a time where the demands on the individual to exist in an instant and complex culture have never been greater, we seem less equipped than ever to respond effectively. But Rogers offers some hope. What he sees are clients moving towards this very state of flux; not with trepidation because it is externally imposed, but with a joy of experiencing a profound sense of inner freedom:

> Clients seem to move toward more openly being a process, a fluidity, a changing. They are not disturbed to find that they are not the same from day to day, that they do not always hold the same feelings toward a given experience or person, that they are not always consistent. They are in flux, and seem more content to continue in this flowing current. (Rogers, 1967: 171)

Within counselling, then, there is the opportunity to reconnect with the actualising tendency and the individual's own valuing process, which can lead to an acceptance and embracing of the continual process of change. If the client can re-establish an openness to experience they can begin to make sense of who they are and, perhaps, be content with the person they discover themselves to be. But in doing so they will have to contend with the dual encumbrance of postmodern living: the undermining of self-acceptance through the external conditions of worth portrayed by the media and the confusion engendered by the uncertainty as to what is real and true.

Summary

The transition from modernism to postmodernism has transformed the landscape in which the person of today has to function. The notion of a single truth obtainable through human knowledge has been discredited, and while for many this remains a potential salvation, the certainty that accompanied such claims has been irrevocably shaken. With the influence of the media dramatically increased, it is almost impossible for the person of today to navigate a path through the real and the unreal. For the client of today trying to be themselves the media presents many powerful and seductive images of what a person *should* be; for anyone struggling to reconnect with their own sense of self, this can be highly confusing and anxiety-provoking.

Thus the challenge facing today's client is to be able to make and maintain contact with their own inner valuing process when the external conditions of worth, at least in relation to the role of the media, have never been more powerful and bewildering. Of hope to the client, though, is Rogers' view on a person's capabilities for change. If the person is able to reach a state of being open to *all* of their experience through self-acceptance, they will be aligned with the actualising tendency that is present within them and be able to live by their own internal valuing process. This would result in a state of continual change and development that would enable the person to respond to the demands of postmodern living. This will not be easy, though, and Rogers has never suggested that any of us, clients or otherwise, ever completely achieve this process epitomised by the 'fully functioning person'. But the closer the client can become to such a process, the more likely they are to develop in ways that are ultimately fulfilling.

Further reading

Anderson, W.T. (ed.) (1996) *The Fontana Postmodernism Reader*. London: Fontana Press.
This collection offers an excellent introduction to anyone interested in the ideas and themes of postmodernism.

Rowan, J. and Cooper, M. (eds) (1999) *The Plural Self*. London: Sage.
Kvale, S. (ed.) (1992) *Psychology and Postmodernism*. London: Sage.
These collections also offer a stimulating mix of views and discussions for anyone interested in reading about the self in the postmodern context.

Rogers, C.R. (1967) *On Becoming a Person: A Therapist's View of Psychotherapy*. London: Constable. (First published 1961.)
Several of Rogers' texts have relevance to the issues of postmodernism but this book perhaps contains the most pertinent extracts.

References

Anderson, W.T. (ed.) (1996) *The Fontana Postmodernism Reader*. London: Fontana Press.

Appignanesi, R. and Garratt, C. (1999) *Introducing Postmodernism*. Cambridge: Icon Books Ltd. (Previously published in 1995 as *Postmodernism for Beginners*.)

Baldwin, M. (2000) 'Interview with Carl Rogers on the Use of the Self in Therapy' in M. Baldwin (ed.), *The Use of the Self in Therapy*, 2nd edition. New York: Haworth Press, pp. 29–38.

Barrett-Lennard, G.T. (1998) *Carl Rogers' Helping System: Journey and Substance*. London: Sage.

Baudrillard, J. (1996) 'The Map Precedes the Territory' in W.T. Anderson (ed.), *The Fontana Postmodernism Reader*. London: Fontana Press, pp. 75–7.

Biermann-Ratjen, E.-A. (1996) 'On the Way to a Client-Centred Psychopathology' in R. Hutterer, G. Pawlowsky, P.F. Schmid and R. Stipsits (eds), *Client-Centered and Experiential Psychotherapy: A Paradigm in Motion*. Frankfurt am Main: Peter Lang, pp. 11–24.

Bohart, A.C. and Associates (1996) 'Experiencing, Knowing, and Change' in R. Hutterer, G. Pawlowsky, P.F. Schmid and R. Stipsits (eds), *Client-Centered and Experiential Psychotherapy: A Paradigm in Motion*. Frankfurt am Main: Peter Lang, pp. 199–211.

Bowen, M. (1986) Unpublished paper.

Bozarth, J.D. (1984) 'Beyond Reflection: Emergent Modes of Empathy' in R.F. Levant and J.M. Shlien (eds), *Client-Centered Therapy and the Person-Centered Approach: New Directions in Theory, Research, and Practice*. London: Praeger, pp. 59–75.

Bozarth, J.D. (1998) *Person Centered Therapy: A Revolutionary Paradigm*. Ross-on-Wye: PCCS Books.

Bozarth, J.D. (2001) 'An Addendum to Beyond Reflection: Emergent Modes of Empathy' in S. Haugh and T. Merry (eds), *Rogers' Therapeutic Conditions: Evolution, Theory and Practice. Volume 2: Empathy*. Ross-on-Wye: PCCS Books, pp. 144–54.

Bozarth, J.D. and Brodley, B.T. (1991) 'Actualization: A Functional Concept in Client-Centered Psychotherapy: A statement', *Journal of Social Behaviour and Personality*, 6 (5): 45–59.

Bozarth, J.D. and Wilkins, P. (2001a) 'Introduction to Volume 3: Unconditional Positive Regard in Context' in J.D. Bozarth and P. Wilkins (eds), *Rogers' Therapeutic Conditions: Evolution, Theory and Practice. Volume 3: Unconditional Positive Regard*. Ross-on-Wye: PCCS Books, pp. vii–xiv.

Bozarth, J.D. and Wilkins, P. (eds) (2001b) *Rogers' Therapeutic Conditions: Evolution, Theory and Practice. Volume 3: Unconditional Positive Regard*. Ross-on-Wye: PCCS Books.

Brazier, D. (1993) *Congruence*. (Occasional Paper no. 28.) Newcastle-upon-Tyne: Eigenwelt Interskill.

Brodley, B.T. (1998) 'Congruence and its Relation to Communication in Client-Centered Therapy', *The Person-Centered Journal*, 5 (2), 83–106.

Buber, M. and Rogers, C.R. (1960) 'Dialogue between Martin Buber and Carl Rogers', *Psychologia*, 3: 208–21.

Cooper, M. (1999) 'If You Can't be Jekyll be Hyde: An Existential-Phenomenological Exploration of Lived-Plurality' in J. Rowan and M. Cooper (eds), *The Plural Self*. London: Sage, pp. 51–70.

Fox, R.F. (1995) 'Manipulated Kids: Teens Tell How Ads Influence Them', *Educational Leadership*, 77 (Sept.).

Freire, E. (2001) 'Unconditional Positive Regard: The Distinctive Feature of Client-Centered Therapy' in J.D. Bozarth and P. Wilkins (eds), *Rogers' Therapeutic Conditions: Evolution, Theory and Practice. Volume 3: Unconditional Positive Regard*. Ross-on-Wye: PCCS Books, pp. 145–54.

Geller, S. and Greenberg, L. (2002) 'Therapeutic Presence: Therapists' Experience of Presence in the Psychotherapy Encounter', *Person-Centered & Experiential Psychotherapies*, 1 (1 & 2): 71–86.

Gendlin, E.T. (1981) *Focusing* (2nd edition). New York: Bantam Books.

Gendlin, E.T. (1996) *Focusing-Oriented Psychotherapy: A Manual of the Experiential Method*. New York: Guilford Press.

Gergen, K.J. (1991) *The Saturated Self: Dilemmas of Identity in Contemporary Life*. New York: Basic Books.

Gergen, K.J. (1992) 'Toward a Postmodern Psychology' in S. Kvale (ed.), *Psychology and Postmodernism*. London: Sage, pp. 17–30.

Greenberg, L.S., Watson, J.C. and Goldman, R. (1996) 'Change Processes in Experiential Therapy' in R. Hutterer, G. Pawlowsky, P.F. Schmid and R. Stipsits (eds), *Client-Centered and Experiential Psychotherapy: A Paradigm in Motion*. Frankfurt am Main: Peter Lang, pp. 35–45.

Gregg, G.S. (1995) 'Multiple Identities and the Integration of Personality', *Journal of Personality*, 63 (3): 617–41.

Hart, J.T. and Tomlinson, T.M. (eds) (1970) *New Directions in Client-Centered Therapy*. Boston: Houghton Mifflin.

Haugh, S. (1988) 'Congruence: A Confusion of Language' in T. Merry (ed.) (2000) *The BAPCA Reader*. Ross-on-Wye: PCCS Books, pp. 62–7.

Haugh, S. (2001) 'The Difficulties in the Conceptualisation of Congruence: A Way Forward with Complexity Theory' in G. Wyatt (ed.), *Rogers' Therapeutic Conditions: Evolution, Theory and Practice. Volume 1: Congruence*. Ross-on-Wye: PCCS Books, pp. 116–30.

Haugh, S. and Merry, T. (eds) (2001) *Rogers' Therapeutic Conditions: Evolution, Theory and Practice. Volume 2: Empathy*. Ross-on-Wye: PCCS Books.

Hawking, S. (1988) *A Brief History of Time: From the Big Bang to Black Holes*. London: Bantam Press.

Hendricks, M.H. (2001) 'An Experiential Version of Unconditional Positive Regard' in J.D. Bozarth and P. Wilkins (eds), *Rogers' Therapeutic Conditions: Evolution, Theory and Practice. Volume 3: Unconditional Positive Regard*. Ross-on-Wye: PCCS Books, pp. 126–44.

Holdstock, L. (1993) 'Can We Afford not to Revision the Person-Centred Concept of Self?' in D. Brazier (ed.), *Beyond Carl Rogers*. London: Constable, pp. 229–52.

Holdstock, T.L. (1996a) 'Anger and Congruence Reconsidered from the Perspective of an Interdependent Orientation to the Self' in R. Hutterer, G. Pawlowsky, P.F. Schmid and R. Stipsits (eds), *Client-Centered and Experiential Psychotherapy: A Paradigm in Motion*. Frankfurt am Main: Peter Lang, pp. 47–52.

Holdstock, T.L. (1996b) 'Discrepancy Between the Person-Centered Theories of Self and of Therapy' in R. Hutterer, G. Pawlowsky, P.F. Schmid and R. Stipsits (eds), *Client-Centered and Experiential Psychotherapy: A Paradigm in Motion*. Frankfurt am Main: Peter Lang, pp. 395–403.

Josselson, R. (1987) *Finding Herself: Pathways to Identity Development in Women*. London: Jossey-Bass.

Keil, S. (1996) 'The Self as a Systemic Process of Interactions of "Inner Persons"' in R. Hutterer, G. Pawlowsky, P.F. Schmid and R. Stipsits (eds), *Client-Centered and Experiential Psychotherapy: A Paradigm in Motion*. Frankfurt am Main: Peter Lang, pp. 53–66.

Kierkegaard, S. (1941) *The Sickness unto Death*. Princeton: Princeton University Press.

Kirschenbaum, H. and Henderson, V.L. (eds) (1990a) *The Carl Rogers Reader*. London: Constable.

Kirschenbaum, H. and Henderson, V.L. (eds) (1990b) *Carl Rogers: Dialogues*. London: Constable.

Klein, N. (2001) *No Logo*. London: Flamingo.

Kvale, S. (1992a) 'Postmodern Psychology: A Contradiction in Terms?' in S. Kvale (ed.), *Psychology and Postmodernism*. London: Sage, pp. 31–57.

Kvale, S. (ed.) (1992b) *Psychology and Postmodernism*. London: Sage.

Lampropoulos, G.K. (2001) 'Common Processes of Change in Psychotherapy and Seven Other Social Interactions', *British Journal of Guidance and Counselling*, 29 (1): 21–33.

Lao-Tzu (2002) *Tao Te Ching* (Translated by S. Mitchell). London: Kyle Cathie Limited.

Laungani, P. (1999) 'Client Centred or Culture Centred Counselling?' in S. Palmer and P. Laungani (eds), *Counselling in a Multicultural Society*. London: Sage, pp. 133–52.

Lewis, D. (1974) *Constantin Brancusi*. London: Academy Editions.

Lietaer, G. (1984) 'Unconditional Positive Regard: A Controversial Basic Attitude in Client-Centered Therapy' in R.F. Levant and J.M. Shlien (eds), *Client-Centered Therapy and the Person-Centered Approach: New Directions in Theory, Research and Practice*. New York: Praeger, pp. 41–58.

Lietaer, G. (1993) 'Authenticity, Congruence and Transparency' in D. Brazier (ed.), *Beyond Carl Rogers*. London: Constable, pp. 17–46.

Lietaer, G. (2001a) 'Being Genuine as a Therapist: Congruence and Transparency' in G. Wyatt (ed.), *Rogers' Therapeutic Conditions: Evolution, Theory and Practice. Volume 1: Congruence*. Ross-on-Wye: PCCS Books, pp. 36–54.

Lietaer, G. (2001b) 'Unconditional Acceptance and Positive Regard' in J.D. Bozarth and P. Wilkins (eds), *Rogers' Therapeutic Conditions: Evolution, Theory and Practice. Volume 3: Unconditional Positive Regard*. Ross-on-Wye: PCCS Books, pp. 88–108.

Mackewn, J. (1997) *Developing Gestalt Counselling: A Field Theoretical and Relational Model of Contemporary Gestalt Counselling and Psychotherapy*. London: Sage.

Masson, J. (1989) *Against Therapy*. London: Collins.

May, R. (1990) 'The Problem of Evil: An Open Letter to Carl Rogers' in H. Kirschenbaum and V.L. Henderson (eds), *Carl Rogers: Dialogues*. London: Constable, pp. 239–51. (Article first published in 1982)

McMillan, M. (1997) 'The Experiencing of Empathy: What is Involved in Achieving the 'as if' Condition?', *Counselling* 8 (3): 205–9.

Mearns, D. (1994) *Developing Person-Centred Counselling*. London: Sage.

Mearns, D. (1999) 'Person-Centred Therapy with Configurations of Self', *Counselling*, 10 (2): 125–30.

Mearns, D. (2002) 'Further Theoretical Propositions in Regard to Self Theory within Person-Centered Therapy', *Person-Centered & Experiential Psychotherapies*, 1 (1 & 2): 14–27.

Mearns, D. and Thorne, B. (1999) *Person-Centred Counselling in Action* (2nd edition). London: Sage.

Mearns, D. and Thorne, B. (2000) *Person-Centred Therapy Today: New Frontiers in Theory and Practice*. London: Sage.

Merry, T. (1999) *Learning and Being in Person-Centred Counselling*. Ross-on-Wye: PCCS Books.

Mitchell, S. (2002) 'Foreword' in Lao-Tzu, *Tao Te Ching*. London: Kyle Cathie Limited, pp. vii–x.

Moore, J. (2001) 'Acceptance of the Truth of the Present Moment as a Trustworthy Foundation for Unconditional Positive Regard' in J.D. Bozarth and P. Wilkins (eds), *Rogers' Therapeutic Conditions: Evolution, Theory and Practice. Volume 3: Unconditional Positive Regard*. Ross-on-Wye: PCCS Books, pp. 198–209.

Moore, S. (1982) *The Inner Loneliness*. London: Darton, Longman & Todd.

Netto, G., Gaag, S. and Thanki, M. with Bondi, L. and Munro, M. (2001) *A Suitable Space: Improving Counselling Services for Asian People*. Oxford: Policy Press.

O'Hara, M. (2002) 'Heuristic Inquiry as Psychotherapy: The Client-Centered Approach' in D.J. Cain (ed.), *Classics in the Person-Centered Approach*. Ross-on-Wye: PCCS Books (article first published in 1986).

O'Hara, M. and Anderson, W.T. (1996) 'Psychotherapy's Own Identity Crisis' in W.T. Anderson (ed.), *The Fontana Postmodernism Reader*. London: Fontana Press, pp. 166–72.

Orlinsky, D.E. and Howard, K.J. (1987) 'Process and Outcome in Psychotherapy' in S.L. Garfield and A.E. Bergin (eds), *Handbook of Psychotherapy and Behavioral Change: An Empirical Analysis*. New York: John Wiley & Sons, pp. 311–81.

Patterson, C.H. (1984) 'Empathy, Warmth, and Genuineness in Psychotherapy: A Review of Reviews', *Psychotherapy*, 21 (4): 431–8.

Polanyi, M. (1958) *Personal Knowledge: Towards a Post-Critical Philosophy*. London: Routledge & Kegan Paul.

Purton, C. (1998) 'Unconditional Positive Regard and its Spiritual Implications' in B. Thorne and E. Lambers (eds), *Person-Centred Therapy: A European Perspective*. London: Sage, pp. 23–37.

Purton, C. (2002) 'Person-Centred Therapy without the Core Conditions', *CPJ Counselling and Psychotherapy Journal* (formerly *Counselling*), 13 (2): 6–9.

Rappoport, L., Baumgardner, S. and Boone, G. (1999) 'Postmodern Culture and the Plural Self' in J. Rowan and M. Cooper (eds), *The Plural Self*. London: Sage, pp. 93–106.

Rice, L.N. (1974) 'The Evocative Function of the Therapist' in D.A. Wexler and L.N. Rice (eds), *Innovations in Client-Centered Therapy*. New York: John Wiley & Sons, pp. 289–311.

Rice, L.N. (1984) 'Client Tasks in Client-Centered Therapy' in R.F. Levant and J.M. Shlien (eds), *Client-Centered Therapy and the Person-Centered Approach: New Directions in Theory, Research, and Practice*. New York: Praeger, pp. 182–202.

Rogers, C.R. (1942) *Counseling and Psychotherapy*. Boston: Houghton Mifflin.

Rogers, C.R. (1951) *Client-Centered Therapy: Its Current Practice, Implications and Theory*. London: Constable.

Rogers, C.R. (1957) 'The Necessary and Sufficient Conditions of Therapeutic Change', *Journal of Consulting Psychology*, 21: 95–103.

Rogers, C.R. (1959) 'A Theory of Therapy, Personality, and Interpersonal Relationships, as Developed in the Client-Centered Framework' in S. Koch (ed.), *Psychology: A Study of a Science, Volume 3. Formulations of the Person and the Social Context*. New York: McGraw-Hill, pp. 184–256.

Rogers, C.R. (1967) *On Becoming a Person: A Therapist's View of Psychotherapy*. London: Constable. (First published 1961.)

Rogers, C.R. (1973) 'Toward a Modern Approach to Values: The Valuing Process in the Mature Person' in C.R. Rogers and B. Stevens, *Person to Person: The Problem of Being Human*. London: Souvenir Press (Educational and Academic) Ltd. (Article first published in 1964.)

Rogers, C.R. (1980) *A Way of Being*. Boston: Houghton Mifflin.

Rogers, C.R. (1984) 'Gloria – A Historical Note' in R.F. Levant and J.M. Shlien (eds), *Client-Centered Therapy and the Person-Centered Approach: New Directions in Theory, Research and Practice*. New York: Praeger, pp. 423–25.

Rogers, C.R. (1990a) 'A Client-Centered/Person-Centered Approach to Therapy' in H. Kirschenbaum and V.L. Henderson (eds), *The Carl Rogers Reader*. London: Constable, pp. 135–52. (Article first published in 1986.)

Rogers, C.R. (1990b) 'Reply to Rollo May's Letter' in H. Kirschenbaum and V.L. Henderson (eds), *Carl Rogers: Dialogues*. London: Constable, pp. 251–5. (Article first published in 1982.)

Rogers, C.R. and Sanford, R. (1984) 'Client-Centered psychotherapy' in H. Kaplan and B.J. Sadock (eds), *Comprehensive Textbook of Psychiatry IV*. Baltimore: Williams & Wilkins, pp. 1374–88.

Rowan, J. and Cooper, M. (eds) (1999) *The Plural Self*. London: Sage.

Sanders, P. (2000) 'Mapping Person-Centred Approaches to Counselling and Psychotherapy', *Person-Centred Practice*, 8 (2): 62–74.

Sanders, P. and Wyatt, G. (2001) 'The History of Conditions One and Six' in G. Wyatt and P. Sanders (eds), *Rogers' Therapeutic Conditions: Evolution, Theory and Practice. Volume 4: Contact and Perception*. Ross-on-Wye: PCCS Books, pp. 1–24.

Sarup, M. (1996) *Identity, Culture and the Postmodern World*. Edinburgh: Edinburgh University Press.

Shostrom, E. (Producer) (1964) *Three Approaches to Psychotherapy*. Santa Ana, CA: Psychological Films.

Sims, J.M. (2002) 'Client-Centered Therapy: The Art of Knowing' in D.J. Cain (ed.), *Classics in the Person-Centered Approach*. Ross-on-Wye: PCCS Books. (Article first published in 1989.)

Spinelli, E. (2000) 'Therapy and the Challenge of Evil', *British Journal of Guidance and Counselling*, 28 (4): 561–7.

Standal, S. (1954) *The Need for Positive Regard: A Contribution to Client-Centered Theory*. Chicago: unpublished doctoral dissertation, University of Chicago.

Stevens, A. (1994) *Jung*. Oxford: Oxford University Press.

Tengland, P.A. (2001) 'A Conceptual Exploration of Incongruence and Mental Health' in G. Wyatt (ed.), *Rogers' Therapeutic Conditions: Evolution, Theory and Practice. Volume 1: Congruence*. Ross-on-Wye: PCCS Books, pp. 159–73.

Thorne, B. (1991) *Person-Centred Counselling: Therapeutic and Spiritual Dimensions*. London: Whurr.

Thorne, B. (1992) *Carl Rogers*. London: Sage.

Thorne, B. (2002) *The Mystical Power of Person-Centred Therapy: Hope Beyond Despair*. London: Whurr.

Tolan, J. (2001) 'The Fallacy of the Real Self', *Counselling*, 12 (2): 18–22.

Truax, C.B. and Carkhuff, R.R. (1967) *Toward Effective Counselling and Psychotherapy*. Chicago: Aldine.

Tudor, K. and Worrall, M. (1994) 'Congruence Reconsidered', *British Journal of Guidance and Counselling*, 22 (2): 197–206.

Van Belle, H. (1980) *Basic Intent and Therapeutic Approach of Carl R. Rogers*. Toronto: Wedge.

Van Kalmthout, M. (1998) 'Personality Change and the Concept of the Self' in B. Thorne and E. Lambers (eds), *Person-Centred Therapy: A European Perspective*. London: Sage, pp. 53–61.

Warner, M.S. (1996) 'How Does Empathy Cure? A Theoretical Consideration of Empathy, Processing and Personal Narrative' in R. Hutterer, G. Pawlowsky, P.F. Schmid and R. Stipsits (eds), *Client-Centered and Experiential Psychotherapy: A Paradigm in Motion*. Frankfurt am Main: Peter Lang, pp. 127–43.

Warner, M.S. (2001) 'Psychological Contact, Meaningful Process and Human Nature. A Reformulation of Person-Centered Theory' in G. Wyatt and P. Sanders (eds), *Rogers' Therapeutic Conditions: Evolution, Theory and Practice. Volume 4: Contact and Perception*. Ross-on-Wye: PCCS Books, pp. 76–95.

Wilkins, P. (1997) 'Congruence and Countertransference: Similarities and Differences', *Counselling*, 8 (1): 36–41.

Wilkins, P. (2003) *Person-Centred Therapy in Focus*. London: Sage.

Wyatt, G. (2001a) 'Introduction to the Series' in G. Wyatt and P. Sanders (eds), *Rogers' Therapeutic Conditions: Evolution, Theory and Practice. Volume 4: Contact and Perception*. Ross-on-Wye: PCCS Books, pp. i–vi.

Wyatt, G. (ed.) (2001b) *Rogers' Therapeutic Conditions: Evolution, Theory and Practice. Volume 1: Congruence*. Ross-on-Wye: PCCS Books.

Wyatt, G. and Sanders, P. (eds) (2001) *Rogers' Therapeutic Conditions: Evolution, Theory and Practice. Volume 4: Contact and Perception*. Ross-on-Wye: PCCS Books.

Yalom, I. (2002) 'Storytelling' (interview with Hanno Koppel), *CPJ Counselling and Psychotherapy Journal* (formerly *Counselling*), 13 (10): 4–5.

HALESOWEN COLLEGE
LIBRARY